PROCEEDINGS OF
THE 2017 INTERNATIONAL CONFERENCE ON
GRID, CLOUD, & CLUSTER COMPUTING

GCC 2017

Editors

Hamid R. Arabnia
Fernando G. Tinetti

CSCE'17
July 17-20, 2017
Las Vegas Nevada, USA
americancse.org

©CSREA Press

This volume contains papers presented at The 2017 International Conference on Grid, Cloud, & Cluster Computing (GCC'17). Their inclusion in this publication does not necessarily constitute endorsements by editors or by the publisher.

Copyright and Reprint Permission

AMERICAN
COUNCIL ON
SCIENCE AND
EDUCATION

Foreword

It gives us great pleasure to introduce this collection of papers to be presented at the 2017 International Conference on Grid, Cloud, and Cluster Computing (GCC'17), July 17-20, 2017, at Monte Carlo Resort, Las Vegas, USA.

An important mission of the World Congress in Computer Science, Computer Engineering, and Applied Computing, CSCE (a federated congress to which this conference is affiliated with) includes *"Providing a unique platform for a diverse community of constituents composed of scholars, researchers, developers, educators, and practitioners. The Congress makes concerted effort to reach out to participants affiliated with diverse entities (such as: universities, institutions, corporations, government agencies, and research centers/labs) from all over the world. The congress also attempts to connect participants from institutions that have **teaching** as their main mission with those who are affiliated with institutions that have **research** as their main mission. The congress uses a quota system to achieve its institution and geography diversity objectives."* By any definition of diversity, this congress is among the most diverse scientific meeting in USA. We are proud to report that this federated congress has authors and participants from 64 different nations representing variety of personal and scientific experiences that arise from differences in culture and values. As can be seen (see below), the program committee of this conference as well as the program committee of all other tracks of the federated congress are as diverse as its authors and participants.

The program committee would like to thank all those who submitted papers for consideration. About 65% of the submissions were from outside the United States. Each submitted paper was peer-reviewed by two experts in the field for originality, significance, clarity, impact, and soundness. In cases of contradictory recommendations, a member of the conference program committee was charged to make the final decision; often, this involved seeking help from additional referees. In addition, papers whose authors included a member of the conference program committee were evaluated using the double-blinded review process. One exception to the above evaluation process was for papers that were submitted directly to chairs/organizers of pre-approved sessions/workshops; in these cases, the chairs/organizers were responsible for the evaluation of such submissions. The overall paper acceptance rate for regular papers was 23%; 14% of the remaining papers were accepted as poster papers (at the time of this writing, we had not yet received the acceptance rate for a couple of individual tracks.)

We are very grateful to the many colleagues who offered their services in organizing the conference. In particular, we would like to thank the members of Program Committee of GCC'17, members of the congress Steering Committee, and members of the committees of federated congress tracks that have topics within the scope of GCC. Many individuals listed below, will be requested after the conference to provide their expertise and services for selecting papers for publication (extended versions) in journal special issues as well as for publication in a set of research books (to be prepared for publishers including: Springer, Elsevier, BMC journals, and others).

- *Prof. Nizar Al-Holou (Congress Steering Committee); Professor and Chair, Electrical and Computer Engineering Department; Vice Chair, IEEE/SEM-Computer Chapter; University of Detroit Mercy, Detroit, Michigan, USA*
- *Prof. Hamid R. Arabnia (Congress Steering Committee); Graduate Program Director (PhD, MS, MAMS); The University of Georgia, USA; Editor-in-Chief, Journal of Supercomputing (Springer); Editor-in-Chief, Transactions of Computational Science & Computational Intelligence (Springer); Fellow, Center of Excellence in Terrorism, Resilience, Intelligence & Organized Crime Research (CENTRIC).*
- *Prof. Dr. Juan-Vicente Capella-Hernandez; Universitat Politecnica de Valencia (UPV), Department of Computer Engineering (DISCA), Valencia, Spain*
- *Prof. Kevin Daimi (Congress Steering Committee); Director, Computer Science and Software Engineering Programs, Department of Mathematics, Computer Science and Software Engineering, University of Detroit Mercy, Detroit, Michigan, USA*

- *Prof. Leonidas Deligiannidis (Congress Steering Committee); Department of Computer Information Systems, Wentworth Institute of Technology, Boston, Massachusetts, USA; Visiting Professor, MIT, USA*
- *Prof. Mary Mehrnoosh Eshaghian-Wilner (Congress Steering Committee); Professor of Engineering Practice, University of Southern California, California, USA; Adjunct Professor, Electrical Engineering, University of California Los Angeles, Los Angeles (UCLA), California, USA*
- *Prof. Louie Lolong Lacatan; Chairperson, Computer Engineerig Department, College of Engineering, Adamson University, Manila, Philippines; Senior Member, International Association of Computer Science and Information Technology (IACSIT), Singapore; Member, International Association of Online Engineering (IAOE), Austria*
- *Prof. Hyo Jong Lee; Director, Center for Advanced Image and Information Technology, Division of Computer Science and Engineering, Chonbuk National University, South Korea*
- *Dr. Ali Mostafaeipour; Industrial Engineering Department, Yazd University, Yazd, Iran*
- *Dr. Houssem Eddine Nouri; Informatics Applied in Management, Institut Superieur de Gestion de Tunis, University of Tunis, Tunisia*
- *Prof. Dr., Eng. Robert Ehimen Okonigene (Congress Steering Committee); Department of Electrical & Electronics Engineering, Faculty of Engineering and Technology, Ambrose Alli University, Edo State, Nigeria*
- *Prof. Igor Schagaev; Director of ITACS Ltd, United Kingdom (formerly a Professor at London Metropolitan University, London, UK)*
- *Ashu M. G. Solo (Publicity), Fellow of British Computer Society, Principal/R&D Engineer, Maverick Technologies America Inc.*
- *Prof. Fernando G. Tinetti (Congress Steering Committee); School of CS, Universidad Nacional de La Plata, La Plata, Argentina; Co-editor, Journal of Computer Science and Technology (JCS&T).*
- *Prof. Layne T. Watson (Congress Steering Committee); Fellow of IEEE; Fellow of The National Institute of Aerospace; Professor of Computer Science, Mathematics, and Aerospace and Ocean Engineering, Virginia Polytechnic Institute & State University, Blacksburg, Virginia, USA*
- *Prof. Jane You (Congress Steering Committee); Associate Head, Department of Computing, The Hong Kong Polytechnic University, Kowloon, Hong Kong*
- *Dr. Farhana H. Zulkernine; Coordinator of the Cognitive Science Program, School of Computing, Queen's University, Kingston, ON, Canada*

We would like to extend our appreciation to the referees, the members of the program committees of individual sessions, tracks, and workshops; their names do not appear in this document; they are listed on the web sites of individual tracks.

As Sponsors-at-large, partners, and/or organizers each of the followings (separated by semicolons) provided help for at least one track of the Congress: Computer Science Research, Education, and Applications Press (CSREA); US Chapter of World Academy of Science; American Council on Science & Education & Federated Research Council (http://www.americancse.org/); HoIP, Health Without Boundaries, Healthcare over Internet Protocol, UK (http://www.hoip.eu); HoIP Telecom, UK (http://www.hoip-telecom.co.uk); and WABT, Human Health Medicine, UNESCO NGOs, Paris, France (http://www.thewabt.com/). In addition, a number of university faculty members and their staff (names appear on the cover of the set of proceedings), several publishers of computer science and computer engineering books and journals, chapters and/or task forces of computer science associations/organizations from 3 regions, and developers of high-performance machines and systems provided significant help in organizing the conference as well as providing some resources. We are grateful to them all.

We express our gratitude to keynote, invited, and individual conference/tracks and tutorial speakers - the list of speakers appears on the conference web site. We would also like to thank the followings: UCMSS (Universal Conference Management Systems & Support, California, USA) for managing all aspects of the conference; Dr. Tim Field of APC for coordinating and managing the printing of the proceedings; and the staff of Monte Carlo Resort (Convention department) at Las Vegas for the professional service they provided. Last but not least, we would like to thank the Co-Editors of GCC'17: Prof. Hamid R. Arabnia and Prof. Fernando G. Tinetti.

We present the proceedings of GCC'17.

Steering Committee, 2017
http://americancse.org/

Contents

SESSION: CLOUD SERVICES AND COMPUTING

Measuring SPECjbb2015 Virtualization Overhead and Application Workloads in a Microsoft Hyper-V Cloud 3
John Medellin, Frank Lee, Lokesh Budhi, Spandana Gennepally

Using Smart Contracts and Blockchains to Support Consumer Trust Across Distributed Clouds 10
Stephen S. Kirkman, Richard Newman

Design of an Architectural Framework for Providing Quality Cloud Services 17
Paromita Goswami, Sayantan Singha Roy, Ranjan Dasgupta

Developing Enterprise Applications for Cloud: The Unicorn Application Framework 24
Marek Beranek, Vladimir Kovar, George Feuerlicht

A Rapid Auto-Scaling Mechanism in Cloud Computing Environment 31
Chia-Wei Tseng, Ming-Shiun Tsai, Yao-Tsung Yang, Li-Der Chou

EZPoll: a Progressive Implementation of Cloud-Based Polling Systems 35
Hans Dulimarta

MCloud API For Managing Data in Multi-Cloud Environment 42
Maram Alhafdi, Ahmed Barnawi

SESSION: DISTRIBUTED COMPUTING AND NOVEL APPLICATIONS + CLUSTER COMPUTING

HPC Cluster Management with Open Source Software 49
Fernando G. Tinetti, Leopoldo J. Rios

Group Mutual Exclusion Algorithm for Intersection Traffic Control of Autonomous Vehicle 55
SungHoon Park Park, BoKyoung Kim, YeongMok Kim

Cost-Efficiency Comparison of an ARM Cluster & Intel Server 59
Jaden D. Weiss

SESSION: POSTER PAPERS

Design of a Tool for Analyzing Supercomputer Status using a Integrated Log Repository 65
Sung-Jun Kim, Jae-Kook Lee, Tae-Young Hong

Correlation Analysis of OpenStack Log using Machine Learning Techniques 67
Ju-Won Park, Eunhye Kim

SESSION: LATE PAPERS - DISTRIBUTED AND CLOUD COMPUTING

Evaluating Cloud Auto-Scaler Resource Allocation Planning Under High-Performance Computing Workloads   71

Kester Leochico, Eugene John

A Review of Electric Vehicle Charging Impact on Power Grid   78

Azhar Ul-Haq, Saif ullah Awan

SESSION

CLOUD SERVICES AND COMPUTING

Chair(s)

TBA

ISBN: 1-60132-458-8, CSREA Press ©

Int'l Conf. Grid, Cloud, & Cluster Computing | GCC'17 |

3

Measuring SPECjbb2015 Virtualization Overhead & Application Workloads in a Microsoft Hyper-V Cloud

John M. Medellin*, Frank C. Lee, Lokesh Budhi, Spandana Gennepally

Faculty and Graduate Assistants at the Master of Science in Information Systems Program

University of Mary-Hardin Baylor

Belton, TX 76513-2599, USA

Abstract— Virtualized environments are a valuable component of most modern automation strategies. They allow for creation of logical systems that can be extended to accommodate a variety of needs in the computing community. The critical manager of this flexibility is the hypervisor software; it controls the direction and limitations of the resources available to execute workloads. Hypervisors are available in large varieties both from reputable vendors and the open source community. This paper executes experiments within the Microsoft Stack (Windows 10, Windows Server 2012 R2 and Windows Hyper-V 2016) and measures the incremental overhead added by the virtualization layers.

The flexibility afforded by Hypervisors is not delivered without increase in computing cost. In addition to operating the internals of the Hypervisor software, there are also penalties to pay for virtualization of resources themselves. Virtualization overhead has been studied in a variety of formats but lately, it has focused on determining overhead driven by the impact of workloads on key components; data, network, memory or computation, and how different Hypervisors perform under certain types of applications.

Our paper measures two types of workloads that are common in the retail industry; online shopping (business to consumer or "B2C") vs shopping at the store. We use the SPECjbb2015 benchmark suite to configure different workload characteristics under each scenario and determine workload and overhead effects using the standard Microsoft stack. Our conclusions indicate that there are differences in overhead incurred by the virtualization layers and between the application workloads themselves. There seems to be an incremental combined overhead/workload penalty for more complex applications. The preliminary conclusion is that this virtualized environment gives better performance benchmarks to online shopping than to traditional store level sales based on the different complexities in the applications.

Keywords— **Hypervisors, B2B/B2C, Application Workloads, Retail Applications, SPEC Corporation, Microsoft Windows 10, Microsoft Windows Server 2012 R2, Microsoft Hyper-V 2016, Services Oriented Architecture, SOA**

I. INTRODUCTION

Virtualized environments were first introduced in the 1970s as a means to extend processing cycle usage and avoid unacceptable levels of idle CPU resources. This concept has been further exploited in the past decade with the advent of Cloud environments. In the Cloud, we are able to model a variety of logical configurations that can help us achieve certain workloads depending on their characteristics [11]. We can adapt our architectures to take advantage of certain configurations that can lend better performance to different types of application complexity.

A significant amount of work has been done in measuring the impact of workloads on the managers of Cloud environments. These managers (Virtual Machine Managers) are also called "Hypervisors". Hypervisors are available both from traditional vendors (Microsoft in the Hyper-V product for example [5]) or on open source (like the OpenStack product [10]). These Hypervisors can lie on the bare-metal (right on the actual hardware) or as extensions to Network Operating systems as in Microsoft Hyper-V being an extension of Microsoft Windows Server 2012 Release 2. These configurations allow the deployment of "client" operating systems which are resident inside the virtual machines (for example a client-based Windows 10 implementation) and provide the execution environment for the applications themselves.

Most of the recent body of knowledge has focused on the measurement of the various parts of the virtualization overhead using standard workload software (these are available suites that focus on producing a type of environment that is stable and has been used in research before). One of these suites is the SPECjbb2015 by www.spec.org. This standard workload generator can simulate a variety of transaction mixes and can enable very complex scenarios of business environments. The system simulates the transaction load of a supermarket chain and can be scaled to multiple supermarkets and multiple "central management" offices. The objective of this system is to measure throughput under an incremental volume scaling algorithm until the system is saturated; the system can no longer keep up with the load provided.

ISBN: 1-60132-458-8, CSREA Press ©

The fundamental objectives of this research are to measure the incremental overhead and workload added by virtualization on two common retail industry application patterns: online shopping and store shopping. We use the SPECjbb2015 to vary the transaction mix between online purchases and in-store purchases for each trial. We start by installing this environment on bare metal versions of Windows 10 and then follow by creating virtual machine images under Windows Server 2012 R2 with the Hyper-V 2016 hypervisor. The reduced throughput reported under each of these Cloud environments is due to the incremental overhead from virtualization. The two differences in workload execution architecture patterns are analyzed through use cases, software architecture patterns and UML activity diagrams derived from the SPECjbb2015 code.

This document is structured as follows:

- We present a summary of the related work that has been done in this area and how we have leveraged those conclusions on our research.
- We structure an experiment which measures the impact of virtualization by first executing the SPECjbb2015 on bare metal under the Windows 10 operating system and then proceed to implement that environment under Windows Server 2012 R2 Network OS with the Hyper-V 2016 Hypervisor. The incremental layer of abstraction is measured and reported by the throughput achieved in the SPECjbb2015 suite.
- We alter the transaction load of SPECjbb2015 to create one scenario with Web Online Shopping ("B2C") transactions and one other with Store ("brick and mortar"; "B2M") sales transactions. The differences in application throughput performance are also reported for each scenario.

This initial research is the first step in understanding the effects of various types of application design patterns for Cloud applications. We believe the differences can be explained (and in further research optimized) by better utilization of standard design patterns in Cloud-based applications.

II. RELATED WORK

Extensive work has been done on the effects of virtualized environments and some of the concepts related to creating virtual systems date back to the 1980s [13]. The full virtual cloud concept was only possible after the creation of software-defined systems that managed servers, storage, network, CPU and other resources known as Virtual Machine Monitors or more commonly as hypervisors [3]. The hypervisor establishes policies for sourcing of resources to the various processes that are resident on a particular infrastructure. Hypervisors are usually complemented by other software to create a Cloud Management Platforms (CMP) that enhance management of the virtualized environment [6].

A. Cloud Framework and Hypervisors

Freet, Agrawal, Walker and Badr [6] provide a review of the general characteristics of the CMP that make hypervisors effective. They reviewed Eucalyptus, OpenStack, CloudStack, OpenNebula, Nimbus and Proxmox (all open source CMPs). Their analysis concludes that OpenStack and CloudStack have over 30 times more messages that some of their other competitors (meaning they are more top of mind in the development community). They proceed to review the frameworks in relation to Xen, KVM, Virtual Box and ESX/VMware and requirements for data center virtualization and infrastructure provision. In that study, various types of workloads are varied through each candidate hypervisor and the throughput is reported. We have adopted a similar workload variation approach and report throughput statistics in our methodology.

B. Virtualization Overhead

As mentioned above, virtualization of resources can be a costly proposition. Oi and Nakajima [9] explored the effects of performance loads on the Xen environment vs others. They determined that the performance of Xen could be enhanced in a virtualized environment by adjusting cache sizes in some applications. Although Xen was never able to provide the throughput that Linux could, (both operating on the hardware without other Operating Systems present) it was shown how certain configuration changes could be effected to drive higher throughput in the Xen hypervisor environment. The point of varying configurations impact on workload efficiency is conclusively illustrated in that work. The benchmarking system used was SPECjbb2001 and the effects of Network Interface Cards (NIC) were isolated so the workload could be measured in memory usage and throughput. We have also adopted the SPEC performance suite but with an application development focus on the results.

Al Jabry, Liu, Zhu and Panneerselvam [1] studied the effects of hypervisor overhead along the following resource usage: disk i/o, CPU, memory and VMM (hypervisor). Their tests were conducted using VMware, Virtual Box (Oracle Corporation) and Windows Virtual PC (Microsoft). Their work benchmarked a standard load in each hypervisor environment and used IOzone to quantify load on disk i/o, RAMSpeed to quantify the impact on memory and UnixBench, to indicate the effect on CPU. The residual resource usage is attributed to the VMM (hypervisor) resource. In their conclusion, they note that hypervisor overhead is considerably low on the memory and disk i/o segments while it is much higher on the CPU usage. This

ISBN: 1-60132-458-8, CSREA Press ©

study points to the need to choose hypervisors in relation to the application workload needs and points to the Microsoft solution as being the more balanced of the hypervisors reviewed with those workloads. We incorporated the usage of the Microsoft stack into our experiments because of the tight integration within itself.

Chen, Patel, Shen and Zhou [2] studied virtualization overhead across multiple VMs running under Xen in cloud environments. They also found that the larger resource usage was attributable to the CPU. They also propose a series of equations that are remarkably accurate in predicting the lateral scaling of workloads on all components based on the observed results of the application under study. Their recommendation for future work is to vary the application characteristics (workload profiles) and further fine-tune their predictive analysis. We incorporate those recommendations by varying our workloads based on B2C and store transaction loads.

C. Application Workload Research

Based on the research referenced, there is a significant impact on utilization of CPU from the overhead generated by the hypervisor. Further the impact is based on the type of application that is operating in the virtualized environment. NasiriGerdeh, Hosseini, RahimiZadeh and AnaLoui [8] measured throughput degradation on Web applications using the Faban suite (a web-based workload generator). They simulated the behavior of heavy transactional Web applications that tend to be very network intensive. Their work also measured the effect on memory, disk i/o and CPU. They concluded that a disproportionate difference exists in CPU resources due to the translation of domain addresses. This work further confirms that the principal resource difference is the CPU utilization even when workloads may be more i/o bound (the penalties associated where in finding addresses; a CPU task, not access to the actual addresses in the Web environment; an i/o task). We incorporate this research by focusing on actual compute power utilization rather than network or disk access. The SPECjbb2015 suite is focused on exhausting the compute resources rather than the disk (i/o) or network resources.

San Wariya, Nair and Shiwani [12] focused their research on benchmarking three hypervisors; Windows Hyper-V, VMWare/ESXi and Citrix Xen in three cloud games; 3D Mark 11, Unigine Heaven and Halo. The objectives of their study are to identify which hypervisor was better from a cloud gaming workload perspective. The three performed differently in each category but were mostly lead by the VMWare product. For our purposes however, the HALO benchmark (number of frames per second) is probably the most predictive of workloads that are CPU bound. In this category, Hyper-V performed 7% ahead of VMWare and 57% ahead of Citrix Xen. This was another reason for selection of Hyper-V as the hypervisor for our test suite.

D. SOA Application Design Patterns

Standardized software architecture patterns provide a series of guidelines for developing functionality that is common across a variety of applications [14]. The work in this domain has been futher elaborated in Services Oriented Architecture (SOA) patterns that can be used to overcome certain design dilemmas. Thomas Erl (with foreword by Grady Booch) [4] presents a comprehensive set of architecture patterns that are common in business. These patterns were matched to the two use cases (B2C & store below) and confirmed in the source code of SPECjbb2015.

Workloads can be modeled in a variety of ways in the application architecture and each can achieve their goals in a different way. If we however, standardize those patters with relation to use cases, there is a greater possiblity for the results to be extrapolated by other application researchers in this field. This approach gives a better chance of replication of the results for other studies relying on our work.

A frequently used SOA application design pattern for abstracting logic from traditional application design nomenclature is shown in Figure 1 below [4]. Other SOA design patterns were confirmed in the implementation of the use cases below in the application code itself.

Figure 1: from traditional design pattern to services architecture design pattern (Erl et. al.)

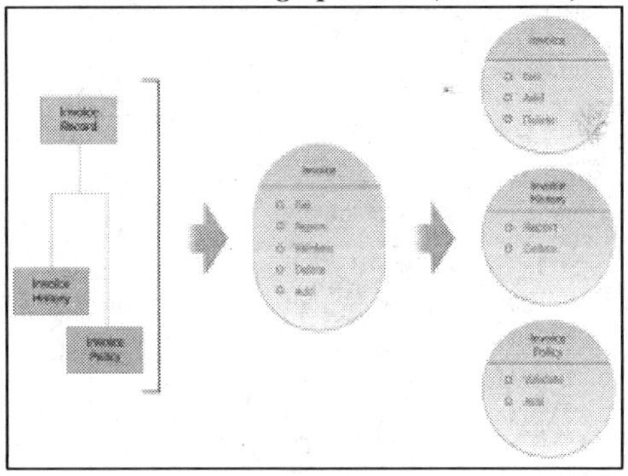

E. The SPEC Benchmarking Suite

The SPECjbb2015 (Figure 4) constitutes a Business to Consumer and Store to Consumer simulation for a Supermarket Chain. The model can be extended to include several supermarkets and several central offices in a variety of virtual machine settings. The benchmarking suite can be configured in a variety of business transaction settings so that different business patterns can be simulated (e.g., web sales versus physical store sales). The system is owned and licensed by spec.org [15] which is a consortium of major IT companies that have agreed on a set of principles to guide the performance benchmarking process.

The system progressively injects transaction loads into the environment until saturation is reached. A sample output of these results is seen in Figure 3. In that graphic the system begins to stress at around the 5,200 java Operations

Per Second (jOPS) with a range of 5K (median tolerance) to 50K (max tolerance). The system reaches saturation (min tolerance) at around 6,700 jOPS and 60K. We report our results using the total transactions up to saturation. Figure 4 is a graphic representation of the architecture of the system.

Figure 3: Sample SPECjbb2015 Benchmark Output
www.spec.org

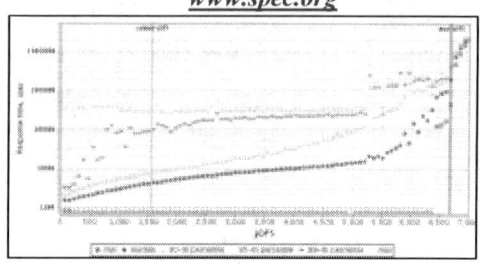

Figure 4: SPECjbb2015 Architecture
www.spec.org

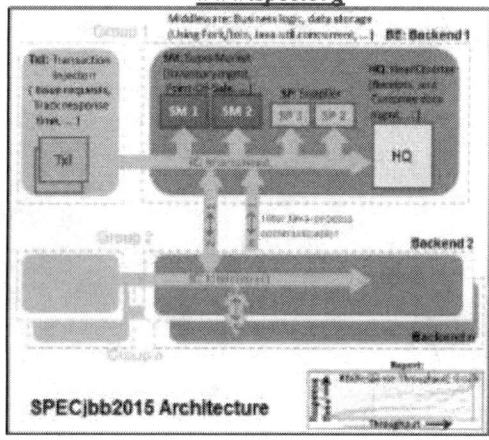

The SPECjbb products have been in existence since the late 1990s and are useful because of their industry acceptance. For example, Karlsson, Moore, Hagersten and Wood [7] used an earlier version (SPECjbb2001) and another application benchmark (ECPerf) to differentiate effects of cache misses between different types of applications.

III. EXPERIMENT DESIGN

As discussed above, experiments were designed where the same application (SPECjbb2015) was installed on:

a) Bare metal with Windows 10

b) VMachine: Windows Server/Hyper-V/Windows 10

Two transaction variations were used; one increased the B2C transaction types to be 90% of the sales while the second one increased the store sales to 90% of the sales.

B. Application Architecture Patterns

The application patterns were analyzed by matching use cases, identifying SOA design patterns and preparing

activity diagrams for each version of the application configured. The details are reported below.

i.   Use Case Analysis

Use cases are a functional decomposition tool that illustrate the process interactions between actors in applications [14]. The processes that we have selected in the SPECjbb2015 suite are fairly standard and follow similar patterns. The use case diagram for the store architecture is similar to this one (www.UML-diagrams.org), the "adornments" in the graphic describe the usage of artifacts.

Figure 5: Store Use Case Diagram

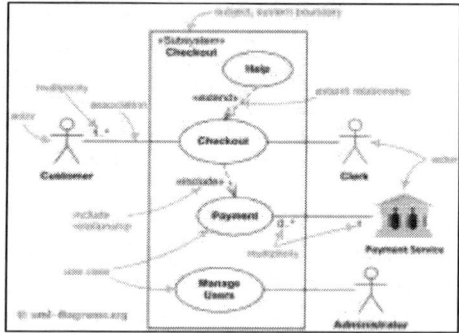

The use case diagram for B2C sales architecture pattern is similar to the one below (www.UML-diagrams.org) :

Figure 6: B2C Use Case Diagram

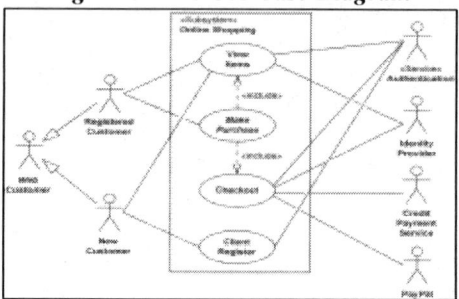

At a high level, both use cases are similar in providing functionality for the user to execute a purchase. However, when inspected the code we found that different design patterns and workloads were implemented. Most of these differences are due to the inventory on-hand function at the physical store. If the system detects an out-of-stock condition, it will proceed to cancel and back out the transaction. This process will take more resources than fulfilling the order from other stores (as it does in the B2C scenario) because it has to place the order items into inventory and invalidate the order itself (error exception in the store UML activity diagram below).

ii.   SOA Design Patterns in SPECjbb2015

We inspected the code again to determine which patterns were evident. Even though the processes are very similar from a functional perspective, they are less similar from a pattern design perspective. The SOA design patterns that were used (in our opinion) are as follows (from Erl [4]):

Table 1: SOA Patterns by Process Modeled

SOA Pattern	B2C	Store
Agnostic Context	X	X
Canonical Protocol	X	X
Domain Inventory		X
Functional Decomposition	X	
Inventory End	X	
Redundant Implementation		X
Service Data Replication	X	

The SOA patterns used differ in the two modules. These patterns were next analyzed in greater detail and we present those results in the UML activity diagrams [14] below.

iii.   UML Activity Diagrams

UML activity diagrams are a useful tool for analyzing the flow of logic through processes [14]. The following diagrams were created from the code in the application. The B2B diagram has less workload complexity (due to the absence of out-of-stock condition handling) than the store diagram.

Figure 7: B2C UML Activity Diagram

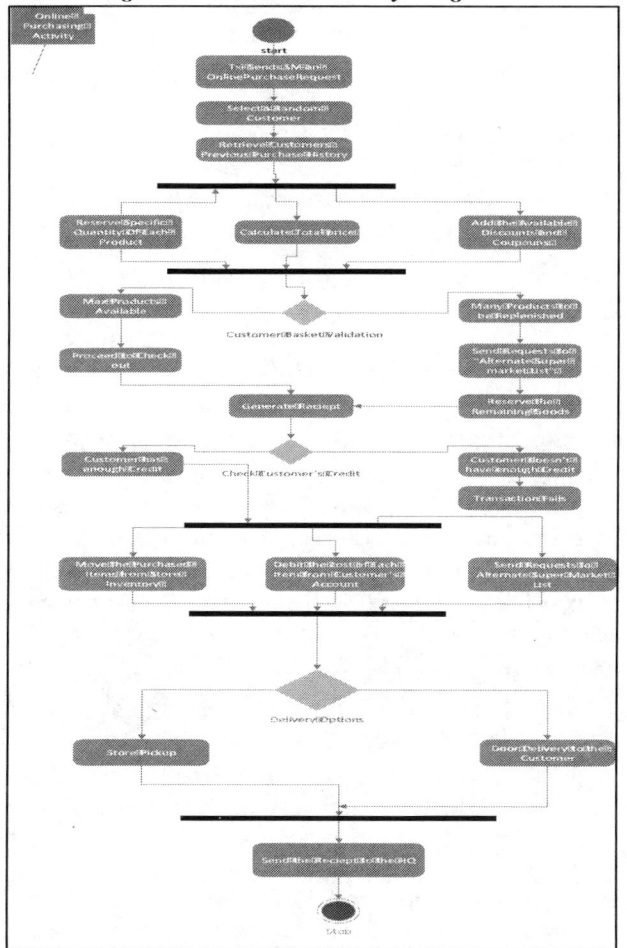

Figure 8: Store UML Activity Diagram

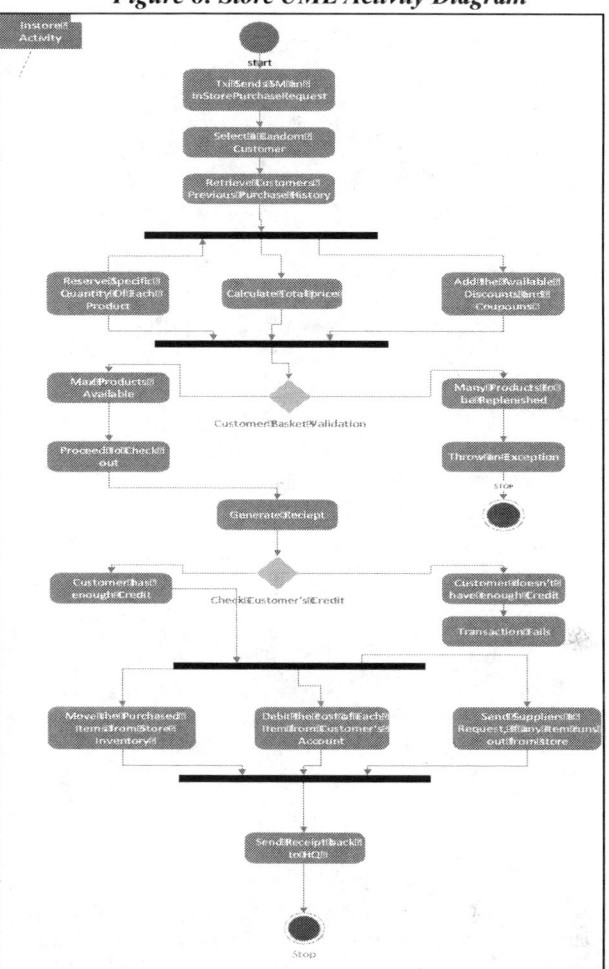

C. Bare Metal Implementations

Two bare metal implementations were used in the experiments. Both were configured to run the SPECjbb2015 suite in a Windows 10 environment. One run of the SPECjbb2015 suite was configured to accept a workload of 90% online "B2C" and 10% store transactions. The other workload was configured to accept the inverse (10% online "B2C" 90% store). No other applications were running in when these tests were executed and the RAM allocated to the processes was 8GB.

D. Virtualization Hypervisor Architecture

The second environment used in the experiment used the Microsoft Windows 10, Server 2012 R2 and the Hyper-V hypervisor extension. The SPECjbb2015 software was compiled inside the virtual machine (VM). A full physical CPU, Network Interface Card (NIC) and all storage available was allocated to the VM. In addition, RAM of 8GB was allocated to make this VM very similar to the "bare metal" configuration. An architecture diagram is shown below, ours however uses only one VM rather than the two shown.

ISBN: 1-60132-458-8, CSREA Press ©

Figure 9: Virtualized Environment Architecture (www.microsoft.com)

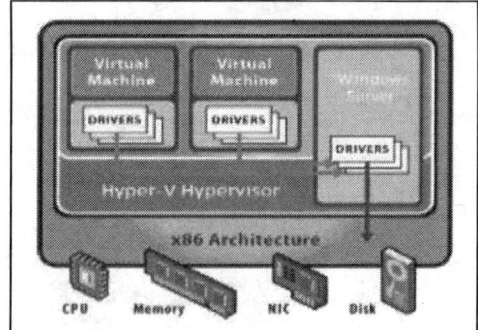

E. Infrastructure (Machine) Specifications

The infrastructure environment that the experiments were executed on had the following specifications:

- Hewlett-Packard Envy 15t
- Intel i6700 quad-core processor
- 16G RAM
- 1TB Hybrid SSD
- 4GB NVIDIA GTX 950M chip

IV.   EXPERIMENT RESULTS

The following graph sets in context the impact of workloads and overhead. When we compare the first two left bars, we observe that the B2C processes more transactions than the store configuration in the bare metal architecture. This is also observed when we compare the third bar to the the fourth bar in the Hyper-V architecture. This is because B2C processes less application workload than the store.

On the other hand, when we compare the first two bars from the left (the bare metal architecture) to the next two bars, we witness the significant effects of overhead on transaction completion due to the impact of the Hypervised environment.

Figure 10: Overall Results

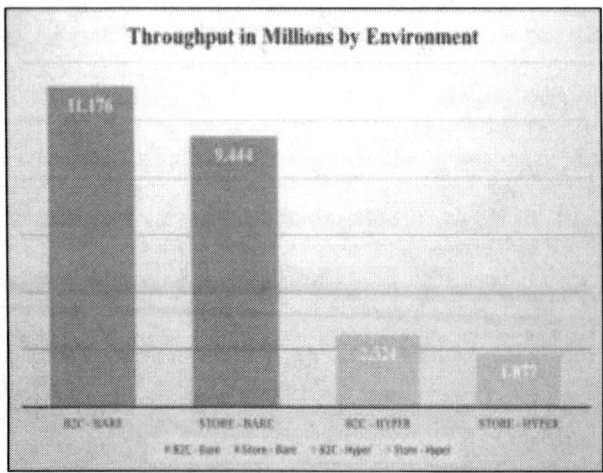

A. Overhead Results

The transaction throughput detail is included in table 1 below:

Table 2: Virtualization Overhead: transactions completed in millions, bare metal vs virtualized

Ap	Win 10	Hyp-V	Diff	% Diff
(1)	11.176	2.524	8.652	77.42%
(2)	9.444	1.877	7.567	80.12%

(Ap) Applications:

(1) B2C

(2) Store

(note: overhead % above is consistent with the 80% penalty observed in other similar implementations; see interpretation below)

B. Workload Results

The transaction throughput detail is included in table 2 below:

Table 3: Application Workloads: transactions completed in millions, B2C vs Store

En	B2C	Store	Diff	% Diff
(1)	11.176	9.444	1.732	15.50%
(2)	2.524	1.877	0.647	25.63%

(En) Environments:

(1) Windows 10 Bare Metal
(2) Win Hyper-V/Sv 2012 R2/Win 10

(note: workload % above is due to additional steps required in the store scenario; see interpretation below)

V.   DISCUSSION & FUTURE PLANS

This article is dedicated to publishing an initial set of results to provide insight into the impact of application architecture on workloads and overhead of virtualized environments. We believe they are easily reproduced because we have used very controlled and standardized environments (SPECjbb2015 and Microsoft stacks). We believe significant additional research could be undertaken into the various components presented.

A. Results Discussion

The results of these experiments confirm the notion that expanded application workloads and virtualization overhead have significant impacts on performance of computer systems. On one hand, there is a 77-80% penalty for virtualization alone (table 1). On the other hand, there is a 15% incremental workload in processing store transactions

ISBN: 1-60132-458-8, CSREA Press ©

versus B2B transactions. A reasonable assumption would be that this 15% penalty would hold constant when the environments were virtualized but that is not the case. As has been offered in several of the references, there is still an additional penalty due to the additional virtual address translation that occurs inside an application process to find the objects that are impacted in order to process them. In this case, that incremental (mixed overhead/workload) impact is significant, around 2/3 of the original workload difference (from 15% to 25%).

At some point in time, the virtualization overhead becomes the minor component if no additional virtual machines are created and the load is significantly scaled. It is hard to say when that might be. What might be safe to say at this point is that the point where virtualization might make sense for store transactions could be 2/3 greater than the point of where it makes sense to virtualize under the B2C scenario. This is the major contribution of this article; it is not only the underlined independent workload difference or the virtualization overhead that will yield the answer, rather the combined impact of both variables on the decision to virtualize under scaled conditions.

B. *Future Plans*

At the point of this writing, the project team is busy executing additional work in two areas:

- Executing experiments to isolate the workload effect of the SPEC components on the Windows Server 2012 R2 environment. The objective of this research is to further isolate this particular component and be able to quantify the additional overhead in this network operating system.

- Identifying a set of tuning principles either in the Windows 10 or the combined Hyper-V environment to deliver higher performance depending on the application workload being executed. The objective of this research is to provide practical recommendations to practitioners with this stack that are executing either the B2C or store environment in their own systems.

In addition, once that work is concluded, the next phase of research will focus on "laterally" scaling the environments. This will entail distributing the SPECjbb2015 components across multiple VM in the same Cloud and reporting similar results. Finally, the suite could be further laterally scaled to ocupy various VM in several clouds. These architectures would task other parts of the hypervisor, operating system and network components even further.

REFERENCES

[1] H. Al Jabry; L. Liu, Y. Zhu, J. Panneerselvam: "A Critical Evaluation of the Performance of Virtualization Technologies". 9th International Conference on Communications and Networking in China (2014). p. 606-611.

[2] L. Chen; S. Patel; H. Shen; Z. Zhou: "Profiling and Understanding Virtualization Overhead in Cloud". 2015 44th International Conference on Parallel Processing. p. 31-40.

[3] T. Erl; Z. Mahmood; R. Puttini: "Cloud Computing Concepts, Technology & Architecture". c. 2013 Arcitura Education, Inc./Pearson Education, Upper Saddle River, NJ. USA.

[4] T. Erl; w/forward by Grady Booch: "SOA Design Patterns". c. 2009 SOA Systems/Pearson Education, Boston, MA. USA

[5] A. Finn; M. Luescher; P. Lownds; D. Flynn: "Windows Server 2012 Hyper-V; Installation and Configuration Guide". c. 2013 Wiley and Sons, Indianapolis, IN. USA.

[6] D. Freet; R. Agrawal; J. Walker; Y. Badr: "Open source cloud management platforms and hypervisor technologies: A review and comparison". SoutheastCon 2016. p. 1-8.

[7] M. Karlsson; K.E. Moore; E. Hagersten; D.A. Wood: "Memory system Behavior of Java-Based Middleware". The Ninth International Symposium on High-Performance Computer Architecture, 2003. HPCA-9 2003 p. 217-228.

[8] R. NasiriGerdeh; N. Hosseini; K. RahimiZadeh; M. AnaLoui: "Performance Analysis of Web Application in Xen-based Virtualized Environment". 2015 5th International Conference on Computer and Knowledge Engineering (ICCKE). p.258-261.

[9] H. Oi; F. Nakajima: "Performance Analysis of Large Receive Offload in a Xen Virtualized System". 2009 International Conference on Computer Engineering and Technology. p. 475-480

[10] J. Rhoton; J. De Clercq; F. Novak: "OpenStack Cloud Computing Architecture Guide 2014 Edition". c. 2014 Recursive Press, USA & UK.

[11] A. Salam; Z. Gilani; S. Ul Haq: "Deploying and Managing a Cloud Infrastructure". c. 2014 Sybex, a Wiley Brand, Indianapolis, IN. USA

[12] A. SanWariya; R. Nair; S. Shiwani: "Analyzing Processing Overhead of Type-0 Hypervisor for Cloud Gaming". 2016 International Conference on Advances in Computing, Communication, & Automation (ICACCA) (Spring). p. 1-5.

[13] W. Stallings: "Operating Systems: Internals and Design Principles 7th ed". c. 2012 Pearson/Prentice Hall, Upper Saddle River, NJ. USA

[14] C. Larman; "Applying UML and Patterns: An Introduction to Object-Oriented Analysis and Design and Iterative Development (3rd Edition)" c. Pearson Education 2005, Upper River, NJ.

[15] https://www.spec.org

Using Smart Contracts and Blockchains to Support Consumer Trust Across Distributed Clouds

Stephen S Kirkman[1] and Richard Newman[1]

[1]Computer and Information Science and Engineering, University of Florida, Gainesville, FL, 32611, USA

kirkman@ufl.edu (contact author), nemo@cise.ufl.edu

Abstract—*name of conference: LATE BREAKING PAPER. In this paper, we propose to add blockchains as a mechanism to store cloud attestations. Blockchains are: 1) cryptographically auditable, 2) append only, 3) accessible to all, 4) tamper resistant. Blockchains also require no central trust mechanism (hence, no central point of failure). Smart contracts are a recent advance of blockchain technology that allow for more expressive development and control. Our smart contract gives the consumer the ability to query the blockchain for the location of their data and history of its movement between clouds.*

Keywords: Cloud Trust, Cloud Security, Distributed Clouds, Blockchain, Ethereum, Smart Contracts

1. Introduction

There is still significant lack of trust in the cloud.[1][2] *Inter-cloud VM migration* significantly impacts consumer trust in the cloud if our data are moved without our consent.[3][4] Due to multiple organizations joining federated clouds, it is hard to know which organization has control of our data.

This paper represents an extension of our research[5] into a policy framework to express the consumer's desires inspired by ORCON. Originator control access control (ORCON) is about data access and control. We used policies inspired by ORCON as a fundamental design philosophy to tackle trust across distributed clouds. We based our framework on four key components:

1) ORCON policy model to *express* our desires
2) A policy *tag* for the data
3) Verification of data movement in the form of *verifying* attestations.
4) Cloud provider to *willingly* commit to agree to comply with consumers policies and participate in the attestations

In this paper, we propose to add blockchains as a mechanism to store cloud attestations. In particular, we propose the use of smart contracts. Smart contracts are a recent advance of blockchain technology that allow for more expressive development and control. The main contribution of our research is to extend our distributed cloud trust policy framework by using smart contracts to store and retrieve attestations for data movement. These are stored on a blockchain.

The rest of this paper is organized as follows. Section II discusses the background of blockchains. Section III covers a next generation blockchain: Ethereum. Section IV proposes our attestation architecture and tests. Section V discusses our results. Section VI is a discussion on transactions and cost. The remaining sections discuss related work, further research, and wrap up with our conclusion.

2. Blockchain Background

We propose blockchains for attestation storage. Blockchains are: 1) cryptographically auditable, 2) append only (blocks cannot be removed), 3) accessible to all, and 4) tamper resistant. Blockchains also requires no central trust mechanism, hence, have no central point of failure. In a distributed cloud environment, we want to ensure that if data cross organizational boundaries, then they are tracked and there is no way to manipulate any logs when stored.

Blockchains were made popular by Bitcoin.[6] A blockchain is a public ledger that is computationally infeasible to alter once set.[7] Blockchains are formed through one-way hashes; hashes are computationally irreversible. A blockchain may be used as a chronological store of transactions.

For Bitcoin, an electronic coin is defined as a chain of digital signatures where owners can transfer coins using a digital signature and a hash of the previous transaction.[6] This is illustrated in figure 1 from Nakamoto's original paper. The blockchain is comprised of individual hashed blocks. Each block contains information about transactions, a reference to the preceding block, and an answer to a complex mathematical puzzle. The math puzzle is termed "proof of work." The proof of work is used to validate the data in the block and is the consensus mechanism used to determine the validity of a transaction.[8] The block is added after a majority of computers on the network reach consensus regarding the validity of the transaction. The blockchain grows as new blocks are added to the blockchain. Once added, the block can no longer be deleted. The blockchain is stored on every computer in the participating network and is therefore globally visible.

ISBN: 1-60132-458-8, CSREA Press ©

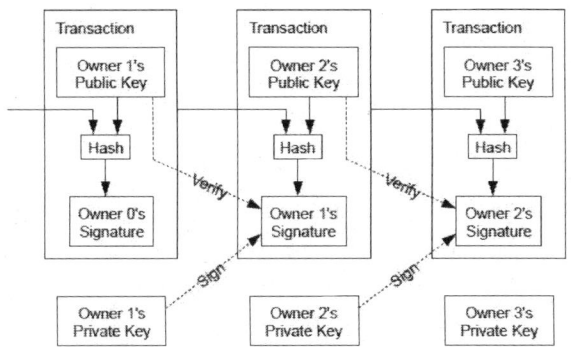

Fig. 1: BitCoin chain of Ownership (From Nakamoto[6])

Proof of work is the driving force behind the creation of the blockchain because it incentivizes people (i.e. miners) to solve complex problems in exchange for digital money. Solving these cryptographic problems serves to verify new blocks to be added to the blockchain. The first miner to solve the problem is rewarded with this currency.[8]

3. Ethereum

We have chosen Ethereum[9] as the blockchain in our research. Ethereum is a next generation blockchain technology whose aim is to build a general trustless ledger with the ability to run programs called "smart contracts." It uses a virtual machine on top of the blockchain called the ethereum virtual machine (EVM). This is a key differentiator from Bitcoin. The EVM is used to run the 'smart contracts' which can be considered transactional programs. It also has a different design philosophy than Bitcoin. "Ethereum is 'Turing complete' meaning that developers can create applications that run on the EVM using friendly programming languages modelled on existing languages like JavaScript and Python."[9]

Payment in the form of gas is required for transactions that change the blockchain. These are paid in units of "ether" (more on this later).

3.1 Smart Contracts

There are two kinds of accounts in Ethereum: 1) those that represent users, and 2) those that represent contracts. Smart contracts are always running on the blockchain once they are deployed; they are essentially programs. They are waiting idle and activated when they receive a transaction or query. Both contracts and users have their own addresses. Once deployed a contract can accept a transaction and manipulate the state of the blockchain. "All transactions (state transitions) are traceable and can be replayed by any node in the system. In fact they are replayed by any node downloading the blockchain from scratch."[10]

The contract is programmed by the developer, tested, then deployed to the blockchain. Smart contracts are both triggered and deployed by a *transaction*. The contract becomes

a permanent part of the blockchain when enough miners have verified the proof of work.

3.2 Attestation Smart Contract

We developed a proof of concept for a smart contract to be used in our proposed attestation framework. Our smart contract is designed to store attestations on the blockchain. Once deployed, this smart contract performs two functions (we envision the potential for more later). One function is activated by the cloud who is storing data movement onto the blockchain. Each transaction changes the blockchain so there are transaction fees. The second function is designed to only report what is stored based on a hash of the consumer's public address.

We used the Solidity[9] programming language. Since Solidity is currently in a state of rapid change, we expect further development on our smart contracts. We used a simulated blockchain that runs on the local computer called testrpc[11]. The flow of work for logging a migration and for querying for attestation proceeds as follows

Cloud:

$$Intercloud.migrate(consumer, CloudB)$$

- Migrate consumer data: $CloudA \rightarrow CloudB$.
- CloudA will send a transaction (associated with the consumer) to the smart contract on Ethereum network.
- The cloud must participate in the Ethereum network.
- When a new block is created by the Ethereum miners, the new transaction will be logged onto the blockchain.

Consumer:

$$Intercloud.getAttest.call(consumer)$$

- When a consumer wishes a data location attestation, they make the request to the contract.
- If the consumer address matches the requested hash, the attestation will be returned, otherwise no data are returned.

There would be no attestation fees to merely read from the Ethereum blockchain. This is termed using a *call*. "When called using *call* the function is executed locally in the EVM and the return value of the function is returned with the function. Calls made in this manner are not recorded on the blockchain and thus, cannot modify the internal state of the contract. This manner of call is referred to as a constant function call. Calls made in this manner do not cost any ether."[12][13]

The code below represents the start of our vision of an InterCloud attestation. We use a dynamic hash table to store consumer data migrations. The consumer blockchain public address is the key for the hash table.

ISBN: 1-60132-458-8, CSREA Press ©

Algorithm 1 InterCloud Migration Smart Contract

```
1: pragma solidity ^0.4.8;
2: contract InterCloud
3: address[] unauthRequest; // Empty Address for Privacy
4: mapping(address => address[]) public attestations;
5: function MIGRATE(address _consumer, address _receiver)
6:     attestations[_consumer].push(msg.sender);
7:     attestations[_consumer].push(_receiver);
8: function GETATTEST(address _consumer) returns(address[] addresses)
9:     if (msg.sender == _consumer) then
10:        addresses = attestations[_consumer];
11:    else
12:        addresses = unauthRequest;
```

Our smart contract only allows a consumer to request information on their own data. We do not store the details of the data, just the fact that data were migrated. However, it should be remembered that the blockchain itself is public; therefore the data that is stored in the blockchain is available for every miner to verify via the Ethereum protocol. At this juncture, we have not built any additional privacy into the contract.

4. Proposed Attestation Architecture

Figure 2 illustrates our proposed attestation architecture. A peer to peer network (in our case Etherum) forms the glue that enables both clouds and consumers to achieve the mutual goal of trust. In order to store attestation information or retrieve attestation information, both the cloud and the consumer respectively must both be a willing participant in the peer to peer network.

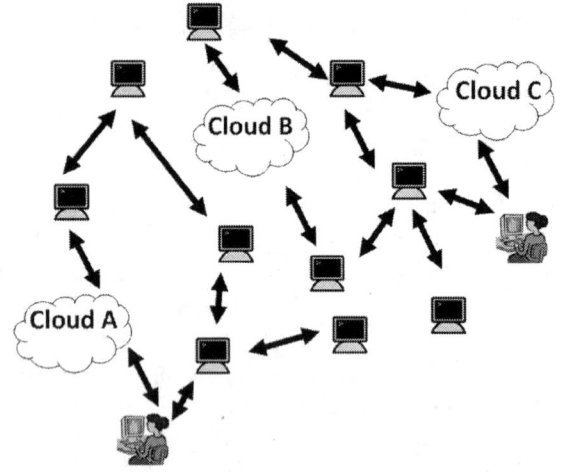

Fig. 2: Attestation Architecture using Ethereum P2P Blockchain

4.1 Smart Contract Testing

For our test hardware, we used a laptop with AMD A8-7410 at 2.2 Ghz with 8Gb RAM. We used the Solidity programming language for smart contracts, the RPC test blockchain, and Truffle development tool.

Table 1: Software and Version

Software	Version	Use
Solidity[9]	0.4.8	Smart Contract Language
TestRPC[11]	3.0.5	Test Ethereum Blockchain
Truffle[14]	3.2.1	Testing & Compiling Environment
Visual Studio Code[15]	1.12.1	Editor
Solidity Online Compiler[16]	0.4.11	Realtime Compiler plus Gas Estimator

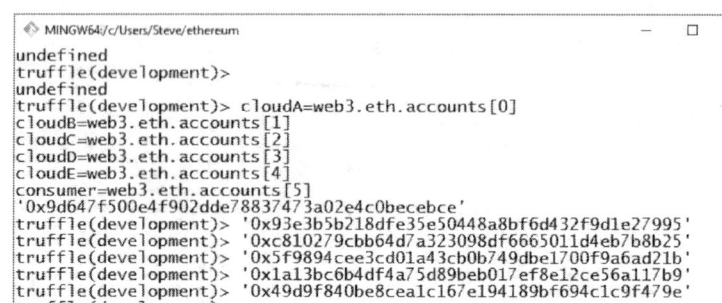

```
MINGW64:/c/Users/Steve/ethereum                    —    □    ×
$ testrpc
EthereumJS TestRPC v3.0.5

Available Accounts
==================
(0) 0x9d647f500e4f902dde78837473a02e4c0becebce
(1) 0x93e3b5b218dfe35e50448a8bf6d432f9d1e27995
(2) 0xc810279cbb64d7a323098df6665011d4eb7b8b25
(3) 0x5f9894cee3cd01a43cb0b749dbe1700f9a6ad21b
(4) 0x1a13bc6b4df4a75d89beb017ef8e12ce56a117b9
(5) 0x49d9f840be8cea1c167e194189bf694c1c9f479e
(6) 0xdfedc405342572211ebd1e3bbb2224b902b5e21f4
(7) 0x241a939de5022e55cf1f51c022f330fc1f33f33e
(8) 0x5732ae8d9ce715d218101f345eb57c23144d0559
(9) 0x51b4bd3d39f8a3236b9ddb3a5baf070906291b84

Private Keys
==================
(0) 56f8d92dc41113af6a2e97dc66cf2724c8a8d10752b104ed7c9781367c6a3bf6
(1) f2b763c4f9f739fb85f832da3a5ba7b5283b7db53adec83f47dc0ed782b4c136
(2) 728b98de64e80ab7f99b613e01e29fdd8f1d3e2136701deac2912543ecdd5b0b
(3) f709560528479899d317508588d101d99b28a92a286ca1aee870a7eba5b2a995
(4) a1b213f8fdda2786ae3056ae1cc3abe25144266126751960320bf4b8c5b38fcb
(5) 56eb718ee882e8790c1d61d0a4d613a92d868b0f36b4e81f104f5f14499b8333
(6) 3e999ea97a1dec708d60b2f9075f9fb2458bc91e947548db2634fd19a3e325b2
(7) c076437d8f7ae01c7fa2e9b24a3216e614c5ce444b60091be46052ed2982969c
(8) c58db197396bafb15a69fb1892292bb859c37181b08cf7214d8a0e215f3c2105
(9) e7d6fb5a77db769a5f25d07c8c6452a16351ef32301979e5b61f1944a4638976
```

Fig. 3: 10 Public Account Addresses - TestRPC

```
MINGW64:/c/Users/Steve/ethereum                    —    □    ×
undefined
truffle(development)>
undefined
truffle(development)> cloudA=web3.eth.accounts[0]
cloudB=web3.eth.accounts[1]
cloudC=web3.eth.accounts[2]
cloudD=web3.eth.accounts[3]
cloudE=web3.eth.accounts[4]
consumer=web3.eth.accounts[5]
'0x9d647f500e4f902dde78837473a02e4c0becebce'
truffle(development)>  '0x93e3b5b218dfe35e50448a8bf6d432f9d1e27995'
truffle(development)>  '0xc810279cbb64d7a323098df6665011d4eb7b8b25'
truffle(development)>  '0x5f9894cee3cd01a43cb0b749dbe1700f9a6ad21b'
truffle(development)>  '0x1a13bc6b4df4a75d89beb017ef8e12ce56a117b9'
truffle(development)>  '0x49d9f840be8cea1c167e194189bf694c1c9f479e'
```

Fig. 4: Cloud Mnemonics with Truffle

4.2 Test Procedures

We used testrpc[11] along with Truffle[14] to test our smart contract. The test blockchain automatically provides 10 accounts. We used these accounts to simulate sending transactions to the blockchain.

We also assigned meaningful cloud names to the addresses for easy reference during our tests. We set the test addresses to cloudA, cloudB, and consumer. Figures 3 and 4 show our mnemonics and default accounts.

To use a smart contract there are two main steps: 1) develop and debug, 2) migrate (deploy) to blockchain. As shown in the following figure, after developing and troubleshooting smart contract code, it is necessary to compile it and deploy it to the blockchain. In our case we deploy it to our test blockchain.

5. Results

In the test run shown in Figure 5 at the end, we deployed the smart contract, ran simulated migrations, and finally executed an attestation request. On an operational blockchain, it would take time for the miners to validate new transactions before attestation data would become available on the blockchain.

Cloud A migrates consumer data to cloud B (assuming the consumer's policy allows it). Cloud A must send a transaction to the blockchain attesting to this. It costs gas for every transaction in a real blockchain. The output from the first command is the receipt from the transaction in the truffle test environment. Note the gas used in the receipt is the estimated cost of gas for the sender. In the second command, another migration is accomplished, this time from cloud B to cloud C. In order to send from different accounts, the truffle environment allows for specifying the sender of the transaction.

In the final commands, a consumer wishes to confirm where their data have been migrated. A consumer issues the getAttest function to retrieve the results, but the request is not coming from the consumer whose attestation is theirs, so this request responds with no data. The second request is coming from the sender whose public address matches the hash into the stored results. The responses from the smart contract represent the raw addresses and do not capture our testing mnemonics. This solution is a first step in a distributed attestation framework supporting cloud trust.

6. Transactions and Costs

Homestead is the first production release of Ethereum. The Homestead[13] documentation explains what a transaction includes: "1) Recipient of the message, 2) A signature identifying the sender, 3) VALUE field - The amount of wei to transfer from the sender to the recipient, 4) An optional data field, which can contain the message sent to a contract, 5) STARTGAS value, the maximum number of computational steps the transaction execution is allowed to take, and 6) GASPRICE value, the fee the sender is willing to pay for gas."[13]

Please note that the wei is the smallest denomination of ether; it is like a micro-penny to a dollar, but smaller. If you use the Ethereum public chain, the network charges a fee for the transfer of ether and any computation steps executed in a contract. By charging for computation, Ethereum discourages attacks and abuse, while subsidizing the overall processing capability and consensus mechanisms of the blockchain (via miners).

Gas and ether are related, but also separate. Gas is strictly a function of computation. Ether is more ambiguous and is a reflection of the free market. "Miners have the choice of including the transaction and collecting the fee or not. If the total amount of gas used by the computational steps spawned by the transaction, including the original message and any sub-messages that may be triggered, is less than or equal to the gas limit, then the transaction is processed. If the total gas exceeds the gas limit, then all changes are reverted, except that the transaction is still valid and the fee can still be collected by the miner."[13] This applies to the Ethereum public chain and is not considered in our tests at this time.

At the time of this research, the Homestead documentation says that using smart contracts for just queries are free; we are guarded about this. This represents the best case in that consumers would not have to pay gas for requesting their attestations. In the worst case, our proposed consumer requested attestations would cost some gas since the primary purpose of gas is for both running contract code *and* making a change to the blockchain. At present, the query is free and demonstrated in our tests.

6.1 An Example

The transaction cost is comprised of two factors:

- $gasUsed$: (fixed) based on computations per contract
- $gasPrice$: (variable) changes with market price of a unit of gas

$$totalCost := gasUsed * gasPrice$$

If we know that the transaction will consumes 3 gas. The approximate cost is calculated using the default gas price (.02e12 wei as of May 2017)[17] would be:

$$3 * 0.02e12wei = 0.6e11wei \text{ (60 billion wei)}$$

$$1ether = 1e18wei$$

Therefore the total cost would be: 0.00000006 ETH $\approx$ 0 BTC $\approx$ \$0.0 (i.e. so small it does not compute).[13][18]

6.2 Our Transaction Costs

These are estimates only. Our test environment provides a simulated $gasUsed$ for each transaction and is based on the computations performed within the smart contract. Our transaction cost $\approx$75,577 gas.

The approximate cost, using the previous gas price would be:

$$75,557 * 0.02e12wei = 1.5e15wei \text{ (1.5 quadrillion wei)}$$

$$1ether = 1e18wei$$

Therefore the total cost would be: 0.0015 ETH $\approx$ .00012 BTC $\approx$ \$.33[13][18]

14

Int'l Conf. Grid, Cloud, & Cluster Computing | GCC'17 |

```
MINGW64:/c/Users/Steve/ethereum                                          —   □   ✕
truffle(development)> InterCloud.deployed().then(function(instance){intercloud=instance})
undefined
truffle(development)> intercloud.migrate(consumer, cloudB, {from: cloudA})
{ tx: '0xc3ccd1e67bf747817b8ae4132303fa59e2130fa180129031a5b55c1ad47f6867',
  receipt:
   { transactionHash: '0xc3ccd1e67bf747817b8ae4132303fa59e2130fa180129031a5b55c1ad47f6867',
     transactionIndex: 0,
     blockHash: '0x34d69b64ed10bb36041ad4b5e0de6da8b23e173e41e3fbc48b09ef16401c8bd3',
     blockNumber: 9,
     gasUsed: 75577,
     cumulativeGasUsed: 75577,
     contractAddress: null,
     logs: [] },
  logs: [] }
truffle(development)> intercloud.migrate(consumer, cloudC, {from: cloudB})
{ tx: '0x12ccdb133e79344b10de15ca54557d2d510667224bb743c68124bfc39ecddc47',
  receipt:
   { transactionHash: '0x12ccdb133e79344b10de15ca54557d2d510667224bb743c68124bfc39ecddc47',
     transactionIndex: 0,
     blockHash: '0x366376972113440a47b576e1ee848eaca0790f367d01e607de15efa7c79ea167',
     blockNumber: 10,
     gasUsed: 75577,
     cumulativeGasUsed: 75577,
     contractAddress: null,
     logs: [] },
  logs: [] }
truffle(development)> intercloud.getAttest.call(consumer)
[]
truffle(development)>
undefined
truffle(development)>
undefined
truffle(development)>
undefined
truffle(development)> intercloud.getAttest.call(consumer, {from: consumer})
[ '0x9d647f500e4f902dde78837473a02e4c0becebce',
  '0x93e3b5b218dfe35e50448a8bf6d432f9d1e27995',
  '0x9d647f500e4f902dde78837473a02e4c0becebce',
  '0x93e3b5b218dfe35e50448a8bf6d432f9d1e27995',
  '0x93e3b5b218dfe35e50448a8bf6d432f9d1e27995',
  '0xc810279cbb64d7a323098df6665011d4eb7b8b25' ]
truffle(development)>
```

Fig. 5: Testing Migration and Attestation Functions

6.3 Advantages & Disadvantages

There are both advantages and disadvantages to using blockchains and Ethereum. For the advantages, we noted that blockchains are append only, public, and tamper resistant. Ethereum's blocks, in particular, are produced much faster than Bitcoin's because they use a different protocol, called Ghost[19], which allows for stale blocks and faster overall block processing. There is debate over the merits of this method which is outside the scope of this research. With regards to security, since the Ethereum Virtual Machine is built on top of the blockchain and it is Turing complete, additional security, privacy functionality might be added. A malicious user might send inaccurate data to the contract (to the extent the contract allows it). Like a cloud, they would still have to pay the transaction fee in order to store bad data on the blockchain.

We summarize the advantages:

- Append only (blocks cannot be removed)

- Accessible to all. Public P2P network.
- Tamper resistant. Block cannot be overwritten just appended
- No central trust mechanism required (hence, no central point of failure)
- Ethereum: Faster creation of new blocks versus Bitcoin, see Ghost protocol[19].
- Ethereum: Added security in the attestation process is possible.

For disadvantages we know that blockchains are made possible by peer to peer networks. However, peer to peer networks are voluntary. Furthermore, the cloud must pay ether for each migration log. This is the price for decentralized trust. There are models that might be used to bring down the cost (e.g. consumer shares load). The cloud could provide misleading data to the blockchain, but it would not benefit them. As a matter of fact, it would cost them.

Therefore, the cloud is incentivized to provide accurate data. It is in their best interest not to provide false information. Furthermore, the account submitting the data are logged into our blockchain storage during a transaction.

These are the disadvantages:

- Participation in the blockchain is not compulsory.
- To send a transaction, it costs the cloud ether.
- Potential for inaccurate data in blockchain.
- The blockchain is public.
- Nothing to impede malicious users from inserting fake data.
- Privacy concerns.

From the advantages listed, particularly the flexibility of running event-based programs on Ethereum compared to other blockchain platforms, we believe Ethereum is the best choice to implement our inter-cloud data migration attestation framework.

7. Related Work

7.1 Blockchains

Other systems have made use of blockchains: Namecoin(DNS)[20], Onename(PKI)[21], and Blockstack[22]. Blockstack tackles some of the shortcomings of previous naming systems like Namecoin. Its main contribution is the separation of the control plane from the data plane and the introduction of a virtualchain. The virtualchain provides the control logic and acts as a gatekeeper to control what gets inserted into the blockchain. This makes it similar to the smart contract. The smart contract, however, takes the abstraction one step higher as it allows for a wider application base.

7.2 Cloud Trust

CloudTrustProtocol[23] allows customers to query the cloud via an API for information related to various service attributes. Rather than query the cloud, our framework provides the consumer the option to state which clouds they trust and which they do not. Cloud Access Security Brokers (CASB) play the role of security middleman between the provider and consumer and consolidating security policy, sign-on, and more. This is a centralized model and the brokers would need to be vetted via a trusted third party.[24] Our model requires no trusted third party and managing the attestations is decentralized. Santos[25] implemented a 'policy-sealed' data trust system for a single cloud domain. It seals (encrypts) and unseals (decrypts) customer data based on the trustworthiness of a cloud node based on the integrity guarantees provided by TPMs. TPMs are trusted platform modules on motherboards designed to provide integrity guarantees at boot time.[26] They do not address trusting the cloud as a whole.

8. Further Research

We plan to research ways to include privacy of the attestations, find more uses for smart contracts in the cloud environment to support trusted computing, and develop more realistic tests. According to Ethereum's creator, Vitalik Buterin, "Because the Ethereum protocol is 'turing complete', it is possible to implement advanced cryptography on top of it."[27] Ethereum is evolving rapidly and we will be able to update our results and smart contracts as this takes shape.

A note on public versus private blockchain:
We will continue to use either a local test environment or a private blockchain. However, our research ultimately supports using the public blockchain because of the inherently distributed trust that public decentralization provides despite the computation and transaction costs. It is possible to use a private Ethereum blockchain in which case Ether is not required.[27] But there would need to be some token value system defined for the private Ethereum blockchain. For further information on public versus private blockchains, see [28],[29].

9. Conclusion

The cloud has an incentive to use blockchain technology for attestation storage because it is inherently trustworthy. Miners might or might not be users of the cloud to enable a synergistic relationship. The accounts held by smart contracts will only fire after receiving a transaction or call. In our case, this would be a cloud provider.[30]

We believe the incentives of using a public ledger will encourage trust in both directions. We experimented with a blockchain to provide for storage of attestations. The nature of attestations demands storing them in a verifiable distributed database that does not reside in the confines of the cloud providing the proof. The blockchain is appropriate for this use.

We have conducted initial tests using an Ethereum contract to track data. The tests are promising, however further tests and improvements are needed as well as research exploring how the market rate of transactions will impact our design. We believe blockchains are a key to decentralized trust in the cloud.

Acknowledgments

This research was conducted with Government support under and awarded by DoD, Air Force Office of Scientific Research, National Defense Science and Engineering Graduate (NDSEG) Fellowship, 32 CFR 168a.

References

[1] "Business trust in data security in the cloud at an all-time low," *http://www.globalservices.bt.com/uk/en/news/business_trust_in_data_security_in_cloud_at_all_time_low*, 2014.

[2] R. Dolan, "Security remains a major obstacle to cloud adoption, study finds," 2015, https://www.datapipe.com/blog/2015/03/25/security-remains-a-major-obstacle-to-cloud-adoption-study-finds/.

[3] Z. ur Rehman, O. K. Hussain, E. Chang, and T. Dillon, "Decision-making framework for user-based inter-cloud service migration," *Electronic Commerce Research and Applications*, vol. 14, no. 6, pp. 523–531, 2015.

[4] C.-H. Suen, M. Kirchberg, and B. S. Lee, "Efficient migration of virtual machines between public and private cloud," in *Cloud Computing Technology and Science (CloudCom), 2011 IEEE Third International Conference on.* IEEE, 2011, pp. 549–553.

[5] S. Kirkman and R. Newman, "Bridging the cloud trust gap: Using orcon policy to manage consumer trust between different clouds," *accepted for publication, IEEE Edge*, 2017.

[6] S. Nakamoto, "Bitcoin: A peer-to-peer electronic cash system," 2008.

[7] M. Pilkington, "Blockchain technology: principles and applications," *Research Handbook on Digital Transformations, edited by F. Xavier Olleros and Majlinda Zhegu. Edward Elgar*, 2016.

[8] A. Wright and P. De Filippi, "Decentralized blockchain technology and the rise of lex cryptographia," *Available at SSRN 2580664*, 2015.

[9] "Ethereum," *https://www.ethereum.org/*, 2017.

[10] A. VanAmmers, *Edgar Guide https://forum.ethereum.org/discussion/2116/in-what-ways-can-storage-history-be-accessed*, 2017.

[11] "Testrpc," *https://github.com/ethereumjs/testrpc*, 2017.

[12] *Ethereum Homestead Documentation http://ethdocs.org/en/latest/contracts-and-transactions/contracts.html#interacting-with-a-contract/*, 2016.

[13] *Ethereum Homestead Documentation Release 0.1 https://media.readthedocs.org/pdf/ethereum-homestead/latest/ethereum-homestead.pdf*, 2016.

[14] "Truffle," *https://github.com/trufflesuite/truffle*, 2017.

[15] "Visual studio code," *https://code.visualstudio.com/*, 2017.

[16] "Solidity online compiler," *https://ethereum.github.io/browser-solidity*, 2017.

[17] "Ether stats," *https://ethstats.net/*, 2017.

[18] "Ether exchange," *http://ether.price.exchange/*, 2017.

[19] "What is the ghost protocol for ethereum, urlhttps://www.cryptocompare.com/coins/guides/what-is-the-ghost-protocol-for-ethereum/ ," 2017.

[20] "Namecoin," 2016. [Online]. Available: www.namecoin.info

[21] "Onename." [Online]. Available: www.onename.com

[22] M. Ali, J. Nelson, R. Shea, and M. J. Freedman, "Blockstack: A global naming and storage system secured by blockchains," in *2016 USENIX Annual Technical Conference (USENIX ATC 16)*, 2016.

[23] C. S. Alliance, "Ctp data model and api, rev. 2.13," *https://downloads.cloudsecurityalliance.org/assets/research/cloudtrust-protocol/CTP-Data-Model-And-API.pdf*, 2015.

[24] CASB, "Cloud access security brokers," *https://totalproductmarketing.com/the-growing-importance-of-cloud-access-security-brokers/*, 2016.

[25] N. Santos, R. Rodrigues, K. P. Gummadi, and S. Saroiu, "Policy-sealed data: A new abstraction for building trusted cloud services," in *21st USENIX Security Symposium (USENIX Security 12)*, 2012, pp. 175–188.

[26] TCG, *Trusted Platform Module http://www.trustedcomputinggroup.org/work-groups/trusted-platform-module/*, 2016.

[27] V. Buterin, *Ethereum in 25 Minutes, Devcon 2 https://www.youtube.com/watch?v=66SaEDzlmP4*, 2016.

[28] *Public vs Private Chain https://blog.slock.it/public-vs-private-chain-7b7ca45044f/*, 2016.

[29] *Ethereum Blog hhttps://blog.ethereum.org/2015/08/07/on-public-and-private-blockchains/*, 2015.

[30] "What is ethereum, urlhttp://ethdocs.org/en/latest/introduction/what-is-ethereum.html?" 2016.

Design of an Architectural Framework for Providing Quality Cloud Services

Paromita Goswami[1], **Sayantan Singha Roy**[2], and **Ranjan Dasgupta**[3]

[1,2,3] Department of CSE, NITTTR, Kolkata, India

Abstract - *Research issues of cloud computing are mainly focused on improving service qualities like better job scheduling, improving uncertainty in completing the job within the given time frame desired by the users, enhancing security etc. As such there exists no framework with suitable policy guideline which can ensure QoS desired for the purpose. In our work, we proposed a tree structure with strong policy guideline for job distribution which will ensure improvement of several such issues like risk management, security, pricing etc.*

Keywords: SaaS; CSP; System model; QoS; Cloud services

1 Introduction

With the proliferation of cloud based services (SaaS, PaaS, IaaS) the issues related to pricing scheme, resource allocation, scheduling, performance predicting, risk management etc. become more and more critical and for particularly medium sized cloud service provider these issues are even more pertinent. A transparent, trusted, secure and reliable service provision is a fundamental pre-requisite for its establishment in the world-wide competitive market. Customers across the world need to depend on the service provider blind-folded. To establish such a trust, beside state-of-art technology, a transparent policy on an architectural framework is a requirement which would be helpful for a scalable, assessable, reliable and easily manageable environment. This in turn will work as a platform to build trust for the customers.

It has also been observed that there exists no policy guideline to cater services to the prospective clients and the service providers, even providing good services, do not have any policy published for such services. In most cases, it follows more towards an ad hoc approach and the offered SLAs [1] eventually become a one-way agreement and very little options are offered to the customer to alter or modify terms and conditions – it becomes a zero-one situation, either accept or reject. In our research work, we looked into various aspects of cloud services and tried to identify an architectural framework among the nodes so that all major aspects of cloud services can be offered in a more transparent manner which include easy options for scalability, smooth resource allocation mechanism, correct performance prediction system, improved resiliency against failure etc.. We here propose a tree structure among the nodes covering a total of 85 systems, which can be scaled up to 341 systems or beyond very easily. An appropriate policy guideline has also been proposed along with the architectural framework. This proposed policy guideline not only helps in efficient management of the resources but also is able to estimate pricing, predictions etc. This model majority caters to SaaS services however can be utilized with necessary modifications for other service types.

2 Related Work

Calheiros et al.[4] have proposed a RMS architecture where the private and public cloud combines to form a hybrid cloud. This ensures better utilization of public resource for dealing with billing users. The core component of this architecture, RMS manages the local resources of the private cloud. This RMS has altogether four parts- Admission control, scheduler, provisioner and accounting. The admission control receives a job execution request from the user. The user also informs QoS attributes in terms of deadline, budget, and files needed for the execution of the job etc. to the admission control. This architecture performs homogeneous as well as heterogeneous tasks. The admission control after receiving this job sends it to the scheduler. The scheduler in turn, checks the required resource, user access right, user's deadline of the job and its available resources. Based on available resources on resource pool, job priority and ownership, scheduler takes a decision about job acceptance. Before accepting the job, the scheduler decides whether it can finish the job within given time frame or not. All the tasks are arranged in such a manner so that scheduler will perform a task at a time and receive new task one at a time. The external queue are acquired for dynamic provision at the time when an external resource is required from the public cloud service provider for the job need to be performed at a fixed amount of time. The amount of extra resource to be used for the execution of the job is decided by the provisioner. The public cloud provider tracks the amount of external resource to be used for the billing system. The billing is done in such a manner that a fixed bill is prepared for the interval. If a task is completed before the billing time, then the provisioner

[1] mcanbu.16@gmail.com

[2] sayantansingharoy@outlook.com

[3] ranjandasgupta@ieee.org

decides if the resource will be reallocated for the next execution of job.

Gholami et al. [1] have proposed a standard "Turnaround_Trust" model which helps to select best source among service provide in heterogeneous cloud. The trust of user is basically depend on reliability, availability, accessibility, security, data integrity, better response time, processor speed, bandwidth etc. This trust model gives better performance than FIFO trust model, QoS_Trust model [8]. In this model, users send their required quality service's attributes and a list of cloud sources to system manager. The selection of cloud sources is done by system discovery under service broker. Based on this QoS requirement the SLA manager gathers the trust values of those resources from trust manager and makes a service level agreement by negotiation with user and selects a best source depending on better response, least turnaround time and fast execution time. Next system manager makes a proper scheduling of resources and resource allocation strategy after a fair discussion with scheduler and resource allocator. At the end of process, Governance service receives that SLA from system manager and prepares a bill of used resource. After that, trust manager is updated by SLA manager with information of trust attributes which comes from system manager and stored in trust history. After sending the processed data from system manager, user tests the processed data and updates trust manager with the data integrity value which is stored in trust history.

W. Lin[2] have proposed a novel resource allocation model for minimum resource (CPU, RAM, BW) allocation in terms of virtual machine in a virtualized datacenter. This model is based on Choco-Based algorithm which ensures to reduce the problem of dynamic allocation of servers and also allocation of Virtual Machines (VM) to the server within an individual time. The fundamental concept of this optimize resource allocation model is to select optimal number of Physical Machines (PM) in a cloud datacenter and allocate all VMs which are working under the selected PMs. The allocation process should follow some rules i.e. (a) PMs must satisfy resource requirement, (b) CPU capacity, RAM, BW of assigned VMs must be less than the remaining CPU capacity, RAM, BW of a physical machine. In static pricing scheme, cloud providers shows the fixed price for using computing resources within a fixed time. Nowadays, cloud service providers offer a dynamic pricing scheme to attract users with low price while using excess computing resources. Dynamic pricing scheme is based on free capacity and workload of cloud providers. Sometimes, a single service provider is not enable to deploy whole service according to user's requirement. They need to split the whole service among multiple service providers and also need to negotiate the price to deploy the part of services with third party service providers. In this paper, authors [3] propose some placement method such as random, round robin, greedy, permutation and first-fit algorithms to find out cost optimal deployment service from multiple cloud service providers. Among those placement methods, permutation method gives best solution by exhaustive search.

The fundamental concept of effective capacity planning is full utilization of physical resource. Jiang et al [7] have proposed an integrated system with intellectual cloud capacity prediction. Based on unique characteristic of provisioning and de-provisioning of virtual machines, this proposed system is able to measure in asymmetric manner the overestimation and underestimation capacity of the system. When existing capacity is less than demandable capacity, the situation of under estimation capacity is arise. Overestimation of the cloud capacity situation arise for idled resources and unnecessary utility costs. One of the most important aim of this model is to predict future capacity while every user's behavior is unpredictable. In this system, real time cloud capacity is measured when a job comes.

In cloud environment, resource utilization depends on right and efficient allocation of cloud resources. A. Ayodele et al. [6] have proposed a service broker policy to enhance the functionality of execution performance of large scale cloud applications on cloud data centers. This service broker policy is based on round-robin algorithm. In cloud service broker policy, service broker is responsible to take a vital decision about choosing a data center to provide an effective service to the user and VM load balancer has the duty of modelling load balance among datacenters. At first, user generates a cloudlet which is referred to service broker via internet for getting the information of datacenter controller. After receiving the information, the user sends request to the datacenter controller and the user request is accepted if VM load balancer finds available VM from the index table. At last, datacenter controller response the user request with a VM ID otherwise it returns null.

3   Scope of Work

So far the research works we reviewed [1-7] it has become apparent that each research work addressed one or more specific aspects of cloud service and tried to improve the same by proposing some additional/improved methods/techniques etc. The same conclusion can be drawn from other works like [18-25] [27-29] without going for individual detailed review. However, like any type of service provider, the success of a cloud service provider lies not only in improving each and every aspect of services, but a consolidated (integrated) approach will also be required so that the customers can expect best of all aspects from a single window. To provide such a holistic service, instead of dealing with piece meal issues, a suitable architectural framework with matching policy guideline is required which can inherently be able to cater a wide spectrum of such services. Our proposed framework will help to provide the customers services like assurance of on-time delivery, zero or minimum failure guarantee, appropriate pricing, post-job security of the raw and processed data, high value trust etc. and will help internally in providing simple resource allocation scheme, efficient job scheduling, performance predicting and

ISBN: 1-60132-458-8, CSREA Press ©

monitoring mechanism, efficient failure handling and overall easily manageable platform.

User gives a job to a Cloud Service Provider (CSP) to execute. If the workload of that CSP increases, CSP distributes the workload to another CSP (all nodes in the system are called as CSP) or among some CSPs and the distribution process is to be continued if workload of CSP is increased. So, the first CSP cannot know (unless a suitable monitoring mechanism is devised in a rapidly changing amorphous environment) where the service is actually run and who is or are executing the job at any instant. Thus for any sort of unstructured, semi-structured or dynamically allocated job distribution mechanism, it becomes extremely difficult to wind up the sub-jobs at the finishing time. In our proposed solution, we operate with a structured and pre-defined job distribution policy where all the CSPs follow the policy for distribution and thus getting back the partially completed results and partial summing up at different stages are possible without much of complexity. We follow a tree structure (quad tree) which distributes the job(s) in a breath first approach and collects the intermediate results in a reverse depth first approach. The tree structure on other hand also provides several advantages in implementing other service features like performance monitoring, higher level of security, transparent pricing etc.

4 System Model

The proposed system model includes major policy guidelines including Architectural Framework, overall processing scheme, job distribution process and quality issues as described below:

A. Major Policy Guidelines

Major guidelines are as follows:

Kind of service Provide: Software as a Service (SaaS)

Members of Cloud Tree Structure: Cloud User, Cloud Service Provider (CSP)

Structure of Cloud: Tree structure as show in Fig. 1

Root CSP has four children CSPs at 2nd layer. Every 2nd layer CSP has 4 CSPs at 3rd layer. So at 3rd layer, total 16 CSPs are present. Every 3rd layer CSP has 4 CSPs at 4th layer. So at 4th layer, total 64 CSPs are present. Therefore, total no. of CSPs in the entire system is 85.

B. Overall Processing Scheme

Initially, a job in the cloud tree structure will be distributed in such a way that each of the CSPs in 4th layer and under same parent CSP (like CSP 29 to 32 in Fig. 1) at 3rd layer performs the same job (with same code and different data set). 3rd layer CSP (say CSP 8) only integrate the job once CSP 29-32 send the result to CSP 8. If more than four children are required to perform a job then 2nd layer CSP will pass the job to more than one 3rd layer CSP. In this case, 2nd layer CSP takes the responsibility to integrate the job coming from different 3rd layer CSPs. However, in this process, some CSPs at the 4th layer may be kept unused for jobs requiring CSPs which are

not integral multiple of 4. Also, a monitoring mechanism (not shown in Fig. 1) will be active at different layers to observe the status of development.

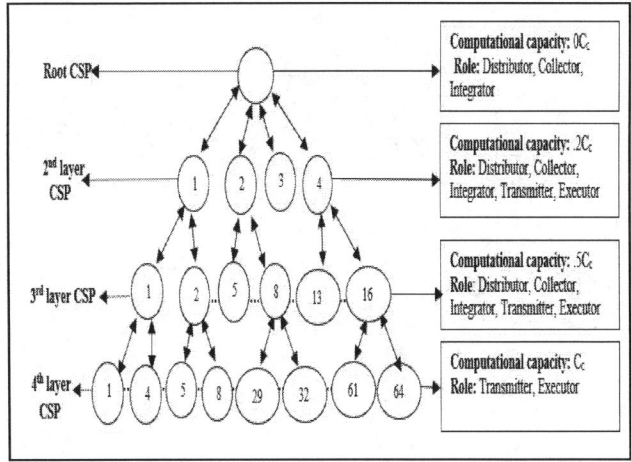

Fig. 1 Architectural Framework of connected CSPs

C. Job distribution process

The distribution process is shown in Table 1. This table is broken down in two parts (i.e. single job and multiple jobs). Decision policies in different scenarios are also described in the table. This description of the decision policy are also referred in Fig [3-6] for graphical representation. Fig. 2 shows the different textures used in Fig. 3-6 indicating different roles.

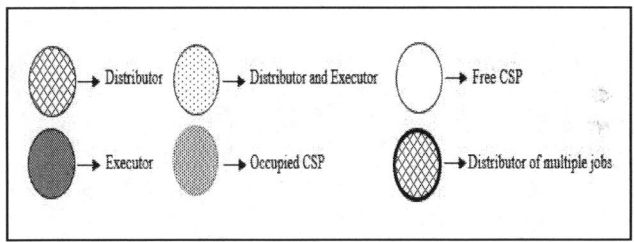

Fig. 2 Texture used to show different roles

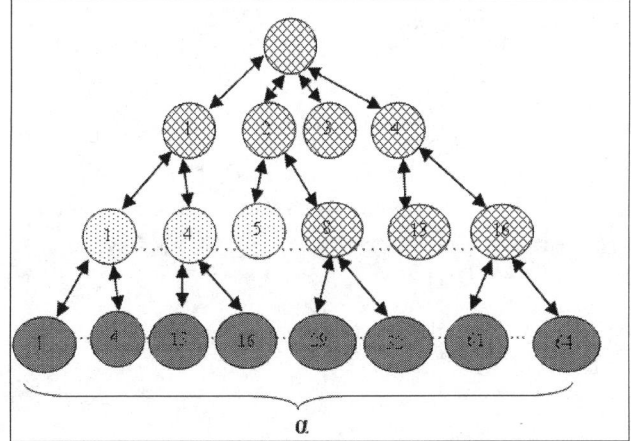

Fig. 3 Job distribution when α =67

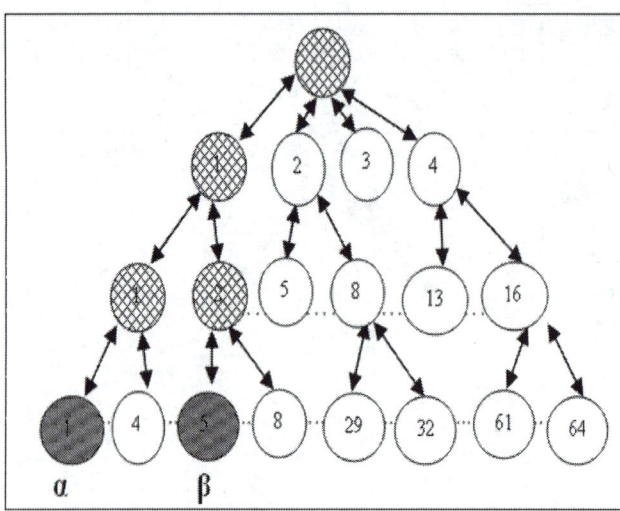

Fig. 4 Job distribution when α < 1 and β < 1

D.   Quality Issues

In rapid growing current business trends, cloud service providers have to face a lot of challenges to fulfill the exact satisfaction level of cloud users while providing and managing services such as capacity planning, prediction, job scheduling and fair resource allocation strategy, performance monitoring, security, risk management, pricing scheme etc. The proposed tree structure job distribution policy ensures the attributes of good quality services to cloud users. In our discussion, we consider several such quality issues (features) which are of prime importance and in the subsequent section, we explain how these features are intrinsically embedded in our proposed model.

Capacity planning: Capacity planning is a mechanism to determine the production capacity needed in order to meet the requirement of user [16] [17]. In the entire system, each CSP has fixed computational capacity for different purposes as defined in major guidelines. Every time the root CSP receives a new job it calculates the required computational capacity to complete the job. After that, root CSP takes a decision

whether the job will be accepted or not which depends on availability of sufficient computational capacity of the system at that instant. Root CSP calculates the required computational capacity for execution by using equation (1). Jobs, for which, the customer's time line cannot be maintained with the existing free CSPs, revised estimated time T_V' ($>T_V$) with existing CSPs may be offered for further consideration.

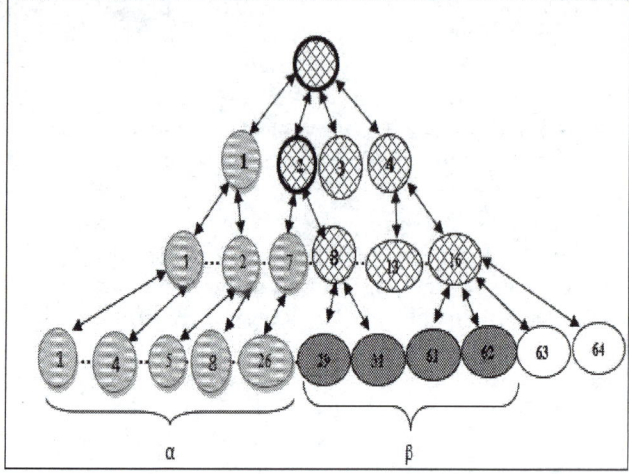

Fig. 5 Job distribution when α = 26 and β = 34 (Fig.4 with added load of β = 34)

Prediction: After applying [15] feasibility test on the receiving job, root CSP can predict the decision of job handling. Using this policy, root CSP can predict number of CSPs needed to complete a particular job. Root can also predict, volume of data the system can handle before running the job which is shown in Table 1. It can also predict the availability of resources after time t, which is primarily a futuristic estimation and can accordingly tune the pricing rate.

Table 1 Distribution policy in different scenario

Job	Initial Work Load (C_c)	Scenario	Required CSP(s)	Check Condition	Remark	Decision Policy
Single job	0	α<1	1	NA	NA	Root CSP distributes the job to first leftmost 2nd layer CSP, this CSP distributes the job to one leftmost 3rd layer CSP and this 3rd layer CSP distributes the job to 4th layer CSP.
		1< α<64	α	NA		Suppose, α = 26, number of CSP required in 2nd layer = Ceiling value of (26/16) = 2 (say, CSP 1, 2), number of CSP required in 3rd layer under CSP 1 = Ceiling value of (16/4) = 4, number of CSP required in 3rd layer under CSP 2 = Ceiling value of (10/4) = 3, The distribution is shown in left portion of Fig. 5 marked as α.

ISBN: 1-60132-458-8, CSREA Press ©

		$64 < \alpha < 72$	$64+[(\alpha-64)*2]$	NA		Let, $\alpha = 67$, no. of CSP required in 2nd layer = Ceiling value of $(67/16) = 5$, in first phase, CSP 1,2,3,4 in 2nd layer get $64 C_c$ eventually, all 64 CSP in 4th layer is occupied. In 2nd phase, remaining, $(67-64)= 3C_c$ is distributed in two 2nd layer CSPs (i.e. CSP 1 and 2), No. 3rd layer CSP works as an executor = ceiling value of $(3/0.5) = 6$ (i.e. CSP 1-6),The process is shown in Fig. 3
Multiple Job	α	$\beta < 1$	1	$\alpha + \beta < 64$	System will accept the job only when initial workload is less than 64 and $(\alpha+\beta)$ must be less than 72.8	Root CSP distributes the job to 2nd layer CSP 1. CSP 1 distributes the job to CSP 2 in 3rd layer as CSP 1 is working on another job. This 3rd layer CSP distributes the job to one 4th layer CSP. This process is shown in Fig 4.
		$1 < \beta < 64$	β	$\alpha + \beta < 64$		Suppose, $\alpha = 26$, $\beta = 34$, α is running in the system as described in Fig. 5. No. of CSP required in 2nd layer = Ceiling value of $(34/16) = 3$ (say, CSP 2, 3, 4), previous job is running on CSP 1 and 2. No. of CSP required in 3rd layer under CSP 2 = Ceiling value of $(4/4) = 1$ (i.e. CSP 8 in 3rd layer) no. of CSP required in 3rd layer under CSP 3, 4 = Ceiling value of $(32/4) = 8$. The distribution is shown in Fig. 5 In this case, CSP 63, 64 in 4th layer will be free and CSP 2 in 2nd layer has to take charge of two jobs.
		$64 < \beta < 72$	(i) $\beta <= 15*4$ (ii)$(\beta -63) <= (15*0.5)$			Let, $\alpha = 1$, $\beta = 65$, α is running in the system. In first phase 4 CSPs get $60C_c$. Remaining, $(65-60) = 5\, C_c$ is distributed among 2nd layer CSPs. So, remaining job is distributed among CSP 1, 2, 3 in 2nd layer. So, CSP 2 to CSP 11 in 3rd layer work as distributor and executor. The process is shown in Fig. 6
			$\beta > 60$, $(\beta - 60) > (15*0.5)$			The system cannot take the job. For further discussion please refer to Risk management section under D of IV.

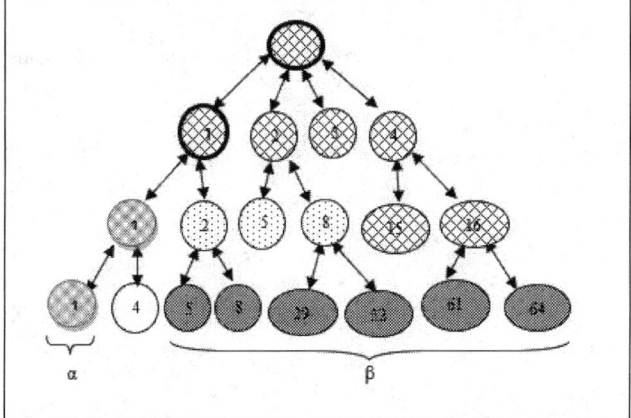

Fig. 6 Job distribution when $\alpha = 1$ and $\beta = 65$

Job scheduling: Job scheduling is a process of assigning jobs to some resources in such a way that balance the load throughout the system. Root CSP plans job scheduling such as completion time of jobs never cross user's deadline. This policy helps to assign parts of a job in its designated resources (i.e. either 3rd layer or 4th layer). The scheduling plan is done before the assignment of job by root CSP.

Fair resource allocation strategy: Fair resource allocation strategy means to assign idle resources of the system with precise manner for executing application software over internet [12]. Root CSP makes job scheduling plan in such a manner that no CSP is heavily loaded nor lightly loaded. In this policy, resources are allocated as per the need of a particular job. But resource allocation is done by following same process for every job. So, this policy is not unbiased in the allocation process.

Performance monitoring: Performance monitoring helps to measure the utilization of resources in system according to different application pattern. So, computing resources of a system can be scaled dynamically to fulfill user's demand [14].The performance of every CSP in the system enhances the confidence level of root cloud service provider to provide continuously QoS services to cloud users. During job execution, root CSP can measure workload and performance of every CSP because it acts as a central controller of the whole system.

Trust: Trust [9] is a core parameter in any types of cloud environment. Using this job distribution policy, our proposed system model keeps trust of cloud users by providing service

ISBN: 1-60132-458-8, CSREA Press ©

within given period of time. Though trust is not a transitive property, it is difficult for cloud users to believe any cloud service providers. In this closed structure, root CSP is the central controller of all decision about job distribution, assignment of jobs to other CSPs, so cloud user can trust root CSP. Suppose, a job is executed in multiple CSPs in 4th layer and job comes from 3rd layer CSP(s). As 4th layer all CSP are disconnected, so there is no chance to interrupt each other from peer level and also not possible from higher level non parent CSP.

Security: It is a most challenging issue in cloud computing technology [11]. Security problem arise when information are transferred from source to destination and malicious attackers are present in the communication links or more than one user use same cloud resources. In this structure, 4th layer CSPs and 3rd CSPs handle only one job at a time and also, no one CSP interacts with other CSPs at the same layer and job is always assigned from parent CSPs, so no two jobs are executed in a particular 4th layer CSP concurrently. 2nd layer CSPs handle more than one job at a time but root CSP always control the 2nd layer CSPs. As the total system is closed and no outsider interrupts the CSPs in different layer, the entire tree structure gives security to cloud users. In every scenario, root CSP work as a decision manager about job distribution in the whole system and root CSP does not borrow external computational capacity from outside provider to execute jobs. So, the total system is secure. Therefore, job execution in every scenario is secure.

Risk Management: In this policy, two types of risk [24][26] are present in terms of job completion time and handling large volume of data. Though, root CSP apply feasibility test on job to calculate required computational capacity to complete the job within user defined time. Depending upon free executional capacity of the system, root CSP takes a decision whether the job will be accepted or not. As long as this calculation holds good, the deadline of user is maintained. However, the calculation may fail, when execution time for large volume of data is not directly proportional to that of small volume as shown in equation 1. The delivery time may also defer because of failure of some of the executing CSPs at 4th layer. However, as there exists a strong monitoring mechanism in the proposed structure, indication for both the cases may be sensed and appropriate mitigation plan can be used. For the second case, the workload (majorly data elements) for the failed system (single failure) may be re-distributed easily to other CSPs of 4th layer under same 3rd layer CSP as they are already executing the same computation. However, for the first risk, the problem is more complex as the time estimation done earlier does not hold good at all and there exists no straight mechanism to estimate the time for such computation in a cloud environment. In such case, historic data, if available may be utilized or may be handled by human intervention, till a suitable model is devised.

Pricing scheme: Pricing scheme helps to get organizational profit from user for providing service [10][13]. Our proposed job distribution policy helps root CSP to calculate a justifiable cost to use cloud computing resources for cloud users. Root CSP can calculate the cost of using resources in its system as 1 unit cost is proportional to computational capacity of each CSP in 4th layer, 1.5 unit cost is proportional to computational capacity of each CSP in 3rd layer, and 1.7 unit cost is proportional to computational capacity of each CSP in 2nd layer. Therefore the standard cost using cloud resource in this tree structure is $(X1*1+X2*1.5+X3*1.7)$ unit cost, where X1 indicates the no. of require CSPs in 4th layer, X2 indicates the no. of require CSPs in 3rd layer and X3 indicates the no. of require CSPs in 2nd layer.

5   Conclusion

Cloud service being the new vehicle for the present and coming decades, researchers all over the world are keen to provide improved services and several tools, techniques, algorithms, approaches etc. are being used and developed towards such endeavors. As lots of big companies are in this business, more and more users are inclined to use the services. A holistic approach is now required to standardize various such service issues like scalability, smooth resource allocation mechanism, correct performance prediction system, improved resiliency against failure. In this research work, we tried to portray an architectural framework with supporting policy guideline which has intrinsically embedded various such critical issues.

6   References

[1] A. Gholami and M. Arani, "A trust model for resource selection in cloud computing environment", 2nd International Conference on Knowledge-Based Engineering and Innovation (KBEI), Tehran, 2015, pp. 144 - 151.

[2] W. Lin, B. Peng, C. Liang and B. Liu, "Novel Resource Allocation Model and Algorithms for Cloud Computing", Fourth International Conference on Emerging Intelligent Data and Web Technologies (EIDWT), Xi'an, 2013, pp. 77 - 82.

[3] W. Li, P. Svärd, J. Tordsson and E. Elmroth, "Cost-Optimal Cloud Service Placement under Dynamic Pricing Schemes", IEEE/ACM 6th International Conference on Utility and Cloud Computing (UCC), Dresden, 2013, pp. 187 - 194.

[4] R. Calheiros and R. Buyya, "Cost-Effective Provisioning and Scheduling of Deadline-Constrained Applications in Hybrid Clouds", in 13th International Conference, Paphos, Cyprus, 2012, pp. 171-184.

[5] I. Foster, C. Kesselman, J. Nick, S. Tuecke. The Physiology of the Grid: An Open Grid Services Architecture for Distributed Systems Integration. Globus Project, 2002.

[6] A. Ayodele, J. Rao and T. Boult, "Performance Measurement and Interference Profiling in Multi-tenant Clouds", IEEE 8th International Conference on Cloud Computing, New York City, NY, 2015, pp. 941-949.

[7] C. Perng, T. Li and R. Chang, "Self-Adaptive Cloud Capacity Planning", IEEE Ninth International Conference

on Services Computing (SCC), Honolulu, HI, 2012, pp. 73 - 80.

[8] P. Manuel, "A trust model of cloud computing based on Quality of Service", Annals of Operations Research, vol. 233, no. 1, pp. 281-292, 2013.

[9] Q. Guo, D. Sun, G. Chang, L. Sun and X. Wang, "Modeling and evaluation of trust in cloud computing environments", in 3rd International Conference on Advanced Computer Control (ICACC), 2016, pp. 112 - 116.

[10] K. Sowmya and R. Sundarraj, "Strategic Bidding for Cloud Resources under Dynamic Pricing Schemes", in International Symposium on Cloud and Services Computing (ISCOS), Mangalore, 2012, pp. 25-30.

[11] F. Zhao, C. Li and C. Liu, "A cloud computing security solution based on fully homomorphic encryption.", in 16th International Conference on Advanced Communication Technology, Pyeongchang, 2014, pp. 485-488.

[12] V. V.Vinothina, and D. Ganapathi, "A Survey on Resource Allocation Strategies in Cloud Computing", International Journal of Advanced Computer Science and Applications, vol. 3, no. 6, 2012.

[13] A. Mazrekaj, I. Shabani and B. Sejdiu, "Pricing Schemes in Cloud Computing: An Overview", International Journal of Advanced Computer Science and Applications, vol. 7, no. 2, 2016.

[14] D. Magalhães, R. Calheiros, R. Buyya and D. Gomes, "Workload modeling for resource usage analysis and simulation in cloud computing", Computers & Electrical Engineering, vol. 47, pp. 69-81, 2015.

[15] H. Chen, X. Fu, Z. Tang and X. Zhu, "Resource Monitoring and Prediction in Cloud Computing Environments", in 3rd International Conference on Applied Computing and Information Technology/2nd International Conference on Computational Science and Intelligence (ACIT-CSI), 2015, pp. 288 - 292.

[16] L. Klosterboer, ITIL capacity management. Upper Saddle River, NJ: IBM Press/Pearson plc, 2011.

[17] M. Rouse, "What is capacity planning? - Definition from WhatIs.com",SearchEnterpriseWAN, 2016. [Online]. Available: http://searchenterprisewan.techtarget.com/definition/capa city-planning. [Accessed: 03- Jan- 2016].

[18] H. Faragardi, R. Shojaee, H. Tabani and A. Rajabi, "An analytical model to evaluate reliability of cloud computing systems in the presence of QoS requirements", in 12th International Conference on Computer and Information Science (ICIS), 2013, pp. 315 - 321.

[19] A. Chowdhury and P. Tripathi, "Enhancing cloud computing reliability using efficient scheduling by providing reliability as a service", in 2014 International Conference on Parallel, Distributed and Grid Computing (PDGC), Solan, 2014, pp. 99 - 104.

[20] W. Li and L. Ping, "Trust Model to Enhance Security and Interoperability of Cloud Environment", in First International Conference, CloudCom, Beijing, China, 2009, pp. 69-79.

[21] W. Chang, H. Abu-Amara and J. Sanford, Transforming enterprise cloud services. Dordrecht: Springer, 2010.

[22] S. Koushik and A. Patil, "Open Security System for Cloud Architecture", ICT and Critical Infrastructure: Proceedings of the 48th Annual Convention of Computer Society of India- Vol I, pp. 467-471, 2014.

[23] S. Tanimoto, C. Murai, Y. Seki, M. Iwashita, S. Matsui, H. Sato and A. Kanai, "A Study of Risk Management in Hybrid Cloud Configuration", Computer and Information Science, vol. 493, pp. 247-257, 2013.

[24] N. Brender and I. Markov, "Risk perception and risk management in cloud computing: Results from a case study of Swiss companies", International Journal of Information Management, vol. 33, no. 5, pp. 726-733, 2013.

[25] C. Garai and R. Dasgupta, "An Improved Job Scheduling Algorithm by Utilizing Released Resources for MapReduce", in 2014 Fourth International Conference of Emerging Applications of Information Technology (EAIT), 2014, pp. 9 - 14.

[26] B. Roy, R. Dasgupta and N. Chaki, "A Study on Software Risk Management Strategies and Mapping with SDLC", in Advanced Computing and Systems for security, 1st ed., R. Chaki, Ed. Springer India, 2016, pp. 121-138.

[27] S. Maiti, C. Garai and R. Dasgupta, "A Detection Mechanism of DoS Attack using Adaptive NSA Algorithm in Cloud Environment", International Conference on Computing, Communication and Security(ICCCS), Pamplemousses, 2015, pp. 1-7

[28] Md H. Ansary, C. Garai and R. Dasgupta, , "An Improved VM Allocation Algorithm by Utilizing Combined Resource Allocation Mechanism and Released Resources in Cloud Environment", International Conference on Parallel, Distributed Systems and Software Engineering, Paris, 2015, pp. 1410-1414

[29] S. Singha Roy, C. Garai and R. Dasgupta, "Performance analysis of parallel CBAR in MapReduce environment," International Conference on Computing, Communication and Security (ICCCS), Pamplemousses, 2015, pp. 1-7.

ISBN: 1-60132-458-8, CSREA Press ©

Developing Enterprise Applications for Cloud: The Unicorn Application Framework

M. Beránek[1], G. Feuerlicht[1], and V. Kovář[1]
[1]Information Technology Department, Unicorn College, Prague, Czech Republic

Abstract - *Modern enterprise applications need to be able to communicate with various types of mobile devices (smart phones, tablets, etc.) and to interact with various types of sensors, controllers and appliances. Another key requirement today is the ability to deploy enterprise applications on a cloud infrastructure. In this paper we describe the Unicorn Application Framework (UAF), a recently introduced framework for the development of enterprise applications at Unicorn. The underlying principles of the UAF include 1) support for cloud deployment, 2) mobile-first - the focus is on supporting mobile application, and 3) IoT-readiness – the architecture enables access for traditional human users as well as IoT devices. The use of this architecture across all projects is expected to improve application development productivity and at the same time minimize the risk of project failures.*

Keywords: Cloud Computing, IoT, Unicorn Application Framework

1   Introduction

Rapid introduction of new software development technologies and methods makes the development of large-scale enterprise applications highly challenging. A number of recent trends that include adoption of cloud computing, extensive use of mobile devices, and the emergence of IoT (Internet of Things) have impacted on the architecture of enterprise applications. Enterprise applications need to be able to communicate with various types of mobile devices (smart phones, tablets, etc.) and provide user-friendly interfaces. In addition to interacting with traditional (human) users, modern enterprise applications need to incorporate interfaces that control IoT devices and are able to receive data from various types of sensors. Today, people access applications mainly through mobile devices, but devices such as televisions and other appliances are beginning to play an increasingly important role in enterprise applications. Unlike traditional enterprise applications that store data on-premise (i.e. on local servers within the organization), most mobile applications store data in the cloud. Data on end user devices (e.g. smart phones, tablets, etc.) are transient (cached) copies of the data that persists on cloud storage. Similarly, application logic is migrating to the cloud enabling applications to be shared by very large user populations. This leaves the presentation layer, i.e. the Graphical User Interface (GUI), as the only application component that runs on end user

devices, taking advantage of the power of the processors designed specifically for efficient GUI support. IoT devices and various appliances contain powerful processors, microcontrollers and input/output interfaces and can receive data and instructions from the cloud.

New types of software technologies and programming languages (HTML5, NoSQL databases, etc.) are becoming popular with software developers. At the same time cloud computing is gaining wide acceptance with organizations taking advantage of reduced costs and scalability associated with public cloud platforms such as Amazon Web Services (AWS), Microsoft Azure, etc. The resulting scenario involves application components deployed on cloud platforms that may involve tens of thousands of users and millions of application components and services that access data stored in multiple distributed data sources.

In this rapidly evolving technology environment, companies involved in software development must ensure high levels of reusability of the software infrastructure and sharing of application components, so as to avoid unnecessary re-development of existing components and improving application development productivity. Equally important is consistent use of system development methods and practices across multiple projects to achieve repeatability of results and to minimize the risk of project failure. Application of manufacturing-like techniques and principles to software development (sometimes referred to as software factory) ensures that software components developed for similar projects are consistently re-used, and that successful methods and techniques are consistently applied on each new project. In practice, this necessitates the use of a standard application architecture that provides basic software infrastructure and methodological framework for application development. Such a framework should facilitate secure and reliable deployment and operation of applications, while taking advantage of the scalability of cloud platforms. In this paper we describe the Unicorn Application Framework (UAF), a recently introduced framework for the development of enterprise applications at Unicorn. In the next section (section 2) we review related literature, in section 3 we describe the UAF architecture, and section 4 presents our conclusions.

2   Related Work

DCE (Distributed Computing Environment) [1] was the first comprehensive industry effort to develop a standard framework that incorporated a toolkit for developing client/server applications, and a range of infrastructure services (Directory Service, Time Service, Security Service, Authentication and Authorization services) and Distributed File System (DFS). A key component of the DCE framework is the DCE/RPC that provides the mechanism for location transparent access for the distributed file system. Following on from the initial efforts to develop a specification and middleware technologies that support application interoperability and provide a range of common services for enterprise applications, IT industry focus has turned to developing a more comprehensive standards-based framework for the implementation of enterprise applications based on the principles of object orientation. The resulting blueprint for enterprise software architecture was the OMG (Open Management Group) CORBA [2] specification. The main idea of CORBA was to specify a common *software bus* (ORB) that provides the infrastructure for the development and deployment of software components and includes a range of infrastructure services (Naming, Transactions, Events/Notifications, and Security services). An integral part of CORBA is the Interface Definition Language (IDL) and the Internet Inter-ORB Protocol (IIOP). CORBA Facilities are services that are sharable across multiple applications and are classified into Horizontal Facilities common to all applications (e.g. email service) and Domain (Vertical Market) Facilities that are specific to a particular industry (e.g. travel). Notwithstanding an extensive effort of most of IT industry leading companies and academia, CORBA has not succeeded in becoming a universal enterprise computing architecture standard. The lack of CORBA success can be attributed to a number of factors, including the complexity of the specification, slow evolution of the specification, differences between CORBA specification and the corresponding vendor products, lack of guidelines for application development, and a poor separation of business components and framework services. Microsoft (www.microsoft.com) has independently pursued the development of a distributed component architecture DCOM [3] and later .Net Framework [4] that form the basis of the Windows family of operating systems. Following the emergence and wide acceptance of the Java programming environment the software industry focused on developing an enterprise software architecture and IDE (Integrated Development Environment) frameworks based on Java. The resulting Java EE specification [5], is a standard specification for a distributed component framework initially developed by Sun Microsystems in cooperation with other leading IT companies including Oracle and IBM. Importantly, the Java EE specification includes a reference implementation and a programming model that provides guidelines for a systematic approach to enterprise software development. Java EE APIs define interfaces to various services such as database connectivity (JDBC), transaction service (JTS/JTA), naming and directory service (JNDI), message

service (JMS), and many others. The Java EE specification includes a specification of the Application Programming Model with focus on role-based development, and a Reference Implementation of the EJB container/server. SOA (Service Oriented Architecture) represents the next step in the evolution of enterprise computing. Many SOA concepts are not new and are integral to earlier generations of distributed computing such as CORBA and Java EE. SOA developments have been driven by technical advances that include commoditization of hardware, Web Services standards and technologies (www.w3.org/2002/ws/) and virtualization. Web Services support has been incorporated into existing IDEs and frameworks typically providing both SOAP and REST interfaces [6].

As noted in the previous section, several recent trends that include the adoption of cloud computing, extensive use of mobile devices, and the emergence of IoT devices have impacted on the architecture of enterprise applications with corresponding impact on application development frameworks [7]. An increasing number of independent software vendors and system integrators are delivering their applications in the form of services hosted in the cloud. According to Raj et. al [8] "The urgent thing is to embark on modernizing and refining the currently used application development processes and practices in order to make cloud-based software engineering simpler, successful, and sustainable." The authors argue that software development has become an inherently complicated task and that a systematic, disciplined, and quantifiable approach is essential to make software development more manageable and to produce quality software products. A related issue concerns the Software Development Life Cycle (SDLC) for cloud-based applications. Adaptation of the software development life cycle for cloud computing has been the subject of recent research interest. According to Krishna and Jayakrishnan to truly benefit from cloud environment, software development teams should look at the cloud computing environment as a new development paradigm and leverage it to lead to differentiated value [9]. Differences between cloud service provider and consumer SDLC cycles have been identified with authors arguing that the shift towards large-scale use of externally provided public cloud services in enterprise applications necessitates re-assessment of the SOA SDLC [10]. The authors describe a Service Consumer Framework (SCF) that incorporates architectural extensions designed to support operation in cloud computing environments [11]. A new requirements engineering process and techniques for capturing cloud-based services was proposed and explained using a large-scale case study based on Amazon Cloud EC2 [12]. While this topic is of current research interest both to academia and industry practitioners, no comprehensive application development framework designed specifically for cloud deployment and incorporating support for mobile and IoT devices is available at present.

ISBN: 1-60132-458-8, CSREA Press ©

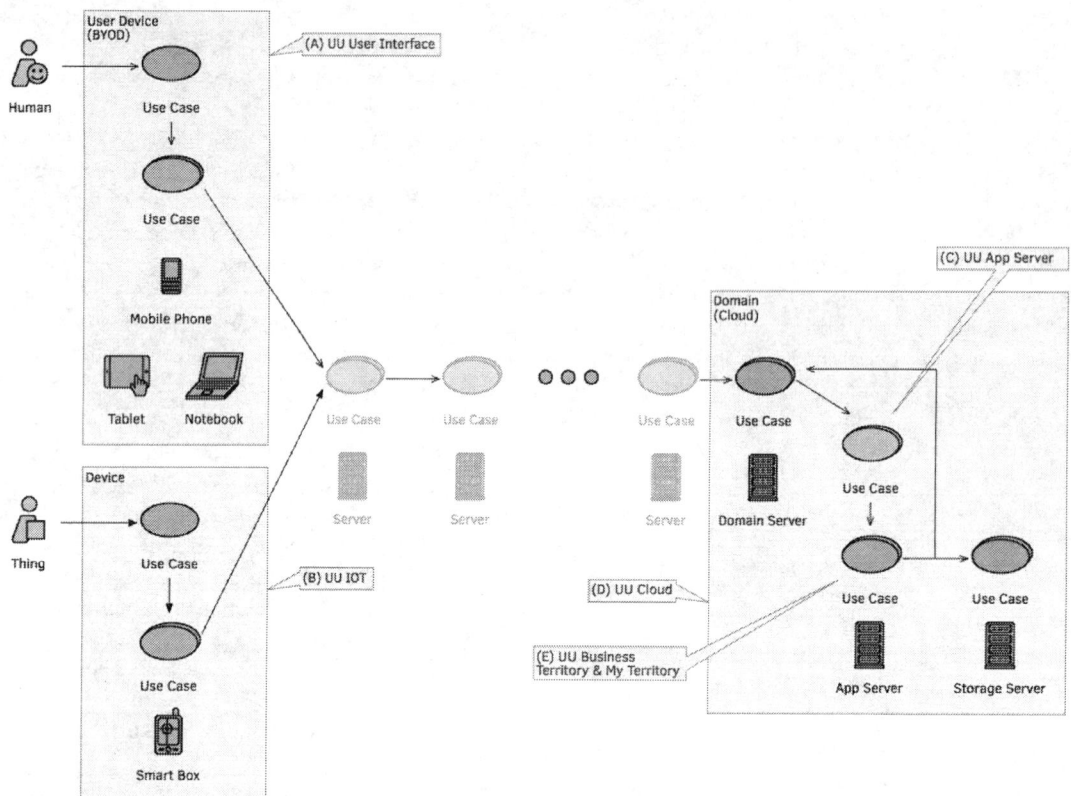

Figure 1: High-level diagram of Unicorn Mobile-first IoT-ready Cloud architecture

3   Unicorn Application Framework

To be effective, Enterprise IT architecture needs to reflect current trends and support cloud deployment of applications, mobile computing and integration with IoT devices. This allows application developers to concentrate on the functionality that directly supports business processes and adds value for the end users. Framework services should enable a single sign-on and user authentication regardless of the physical location of the user (office, home, hotel, etc.) and the application should run on different end user devices such as mobile phones, tablets, notebooks, etc. without the need for excessive modifications. Reusing standard framework services across all projects saves programming effort and improves the reliability of the applications. Unicorn Application Framework (UAF) is a mobile-first, IoT-ready cloud architecture for the production of enterprise applications utilizing standard framework services and minimizing the programming effort. As illustrated in Figure 1, the UAF architecture consists of five key components:

A. *uuUserInterface* - a standard specification and the corresponding framework components for the development of Graphical User Interfaces (GUI) for large range of application requirements that can be deployed on all widely available modern devices, including mobile phones, tablets, notebooks, smart TVs, desktop computers, etc.

B. *uuIoT* - a standard specification and the corresponding framework components that can control a very large number of IoT devices and various appliances interacting with enterprise applications.

C. *uuAppServer* - a standard specification and the corresponding framework components for developing cloud-based application server components that encapsulate application requirements and access persistent cloud storage.

D. *uuCloud* - a standard specification and the corresponding framework components that enable autonomic provisioning of elastic cloud services delivered from a reliable data center that can support very large number of virtual containers and servers.

E. *uuBT and uuMT* - a standard specification and the corresponding framework components that support the development of large-scale information systems for organizations (uuBT) and individuals (uuMT). The systems represent organizations as groups of users with predefined organizational structure and enables access to relevant objects according to privileges derived from the organizational structure.

In the following sections we describe the key UAF concepts and components.

ISBN: 1-60132-458-8, CSREA Press ©

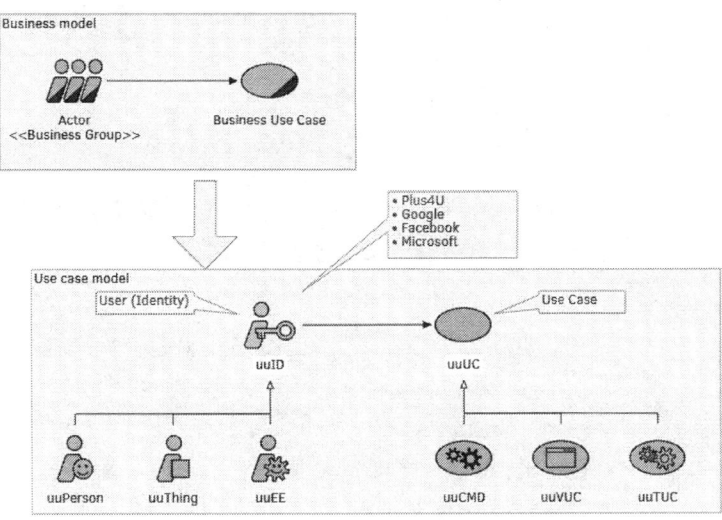

Figure 2: Users and Use Cases

3.1   Users and Use-cases

A central UAF concept is a business use-case - business logic that implements a specific user requirement. When designing applications, the focus is on creating added value through specific business use cases. The UAF framework uses a range of technology standards that implement the bottom (standard technology) layers of the architecture; consistent use of these technology standards provides a solid basis for the implementation of enterprise applications. As illustrated in Figure 2, the implementation of the use cases focuses on three main components that are collectively known as Unicorn Universe Use Cases (uuUC). The use case components share many features and underlying principles, but they are typically implemented using different computer languages and technologies.

A. *uuCMD* - Centralized application logic executed on application servers deployed in the cloud. uuCMD may also include access to persistent data implemented as a separate module.

B. *uuVUC* - Visual Use Cases contain application logic executed on end user devices, i.e. mobile phones, tablets, smart TVs, desktop computers, laptops, etc.

C. *uuTUC* - Thing Use Cases contain application logic executed on various types of IoT devices and appliances (e.g. devices used for home automation, temperature and humidity sensors, etc.)

The UAF architecture defines three types of users: uuPerson (i.e. human users), uuThing (IoT device), and uuEE. The uuEE is an abstract user, for example an application, or a user who is not able to interact directly with the visual user interface (e.g. a disabled person using a specialized UI). Irrespective of the type of the interface and the type of user,

a global identity (uuID) determines the access privileges to UAF application components. uuID can be linked to other widely used identities allowing access using Google, Facebook or Microsoft identities, or government provided user identity, when that becomes available in the future.

3.2   uuApp

UAF architecture defines the concept of uuApp (Unicorn Universe Application) - a component that implements a cohesive set of application functions designed to solve a specific user requirement. uuApp component is consistent with the Unicorn mobile-first, IoT-ready cloud-based approach, and follows the Unicorn principles for developing enterprise applications. UAF provides the environment for the implementation and deployment of uuApp applications.

As illustrated in Figure 3, uuApp applications are composed of application components that implement specific functions; UAF includes the concept of a Sub-Application (uuSubApp) to address this requirement. uuSubApp is an independent unit of functionality deployed on a *logical* application server (uuAppServer) that uses uuAppObjectStore (structured data store, e.g. a relational database) and uuAppBinaryStore (binary data store) libraries to access persistent data stored in cloud data stores. For the purposes of performance management individual uuUC components may be distributed across separate application servers in the form of individually addressable SPPs (Separately Performing Parts). We made an architectural decision to associate each uuSubApp with a single logical uuAppServer to ensure fast access to persistent data (implementing fast connectivity between the application server and the corresponding data source) and to maintain security and consistency of the underlying data sources, ensuring that access to data is controlled via the uuCMD component.

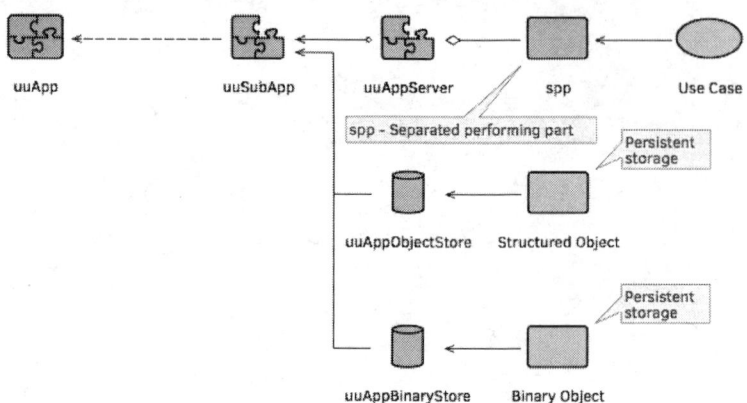

Figure 3: Deployment of uuApp applications

3.3 User Authentication

A key requirement for any application framework is control of access, ensuring that only authorized users can access data and run applications. A typical solution is to introduce the concept of user identity that is associated with an individual user and the concept of a data object as a unit of access. Access rights are then determined by the relationship between user identity, a specific data object, and the type of operation on that object, (i.e. read, write, delete, etc.). However, this model breaks down in cloud/IoT environments as the number of combinations of data objects, applications and users can become extremely large. Our approach has been to determine access right based on user Roles and Artifacts with access rights derived from the organizational structure (i.e. hierarchy of roles) for each artifact/role combination. To facilitate management of user access in large-scale cloud-based environments involving very large number of users and IoT devices we have extended this security model by introducing the concepts of uuAppProfile (a collection of functions of uuSubApp applications) and uuAppWorkSpace (a collection of structured and binary objects), aggregating both sub-applications and data objects according to their use. As illustrated in Figure 4, access privileges are granted to application workspaces (uuAppWorkSpace) according to application profiles (uuAppProfile), reducing the number of possible access privilege combinations.

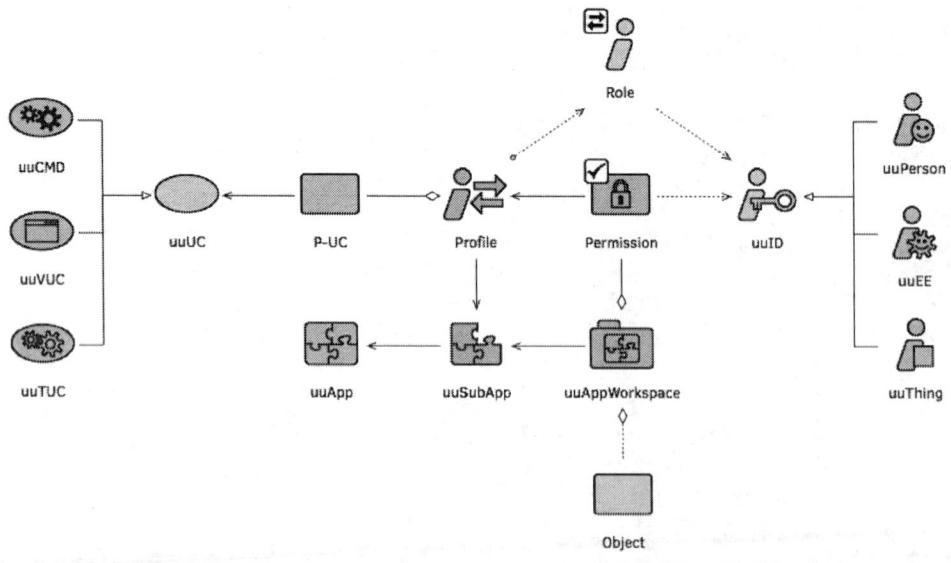

Figure 4: uuApp Security Model

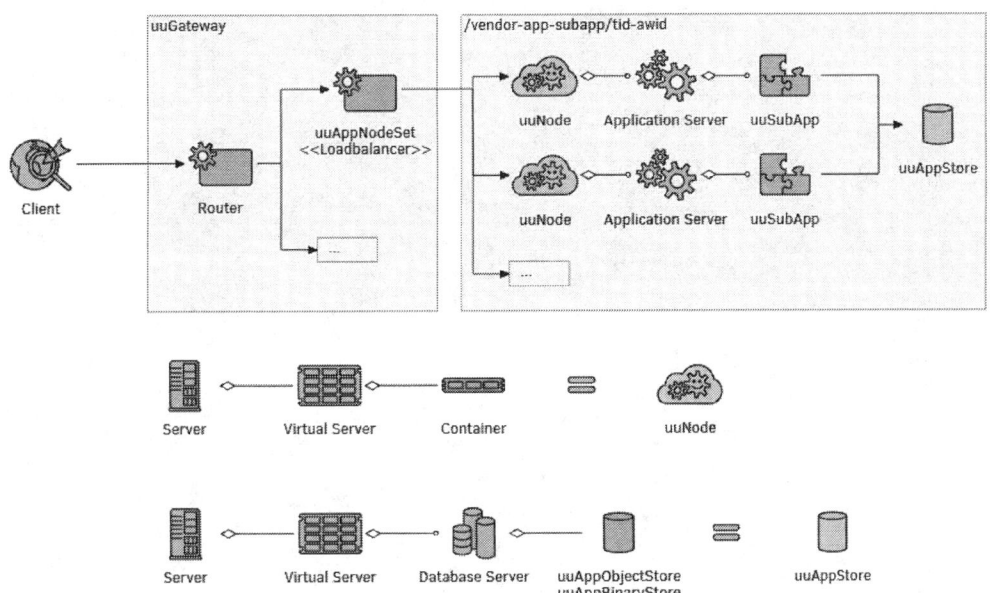

Figure 5: uuCloud Topology

3.4   uuCloud

UAF applications (uuApps) are typically deployed into a hybrid cloud environment (i.e. a combination of public and private cloud) in the form of virtual servers (uuAppServer) packaged as containers (e.g. Docker container: www.docker.com). Containers that encapsulate the entire application component can then be deployed on a public cloud (e.g. AWS or Microsoft Azure) or on a private infrastructure (i.e. on-premise). Individual application servers are addressed using a uuURI via the uuGateway that implements a router and a load balancer to optimize the use of the hardware infrastructure. uuURI is a version of the generic REST URI (Uniform Resource Identifier) adapted for addressing uuApp applications. uuURI uses a standard string format to route the request to a specified gateway (e.g. plus4u.net, AWS, etc.) and to specify which server should execute the application request on behalf of the user, identified by the identity contained in the URI header).

As illustrated in Figure 5, following an uuURI request from a client, the uuGateway router forwards the request to an uuAppNodeSet (a set of logically identical servers replicating the uuSubApp functionality). As the implementation of uuSubApp is stateless the uuAppNodeSet load balancer dynamically deploys relevant containers to optimize overall performance of the application and to provide a failover capability. Individual containers are typically deployed on a public cloud infrastructure (e.g. Amazon AWS) and access data from cloud-based data stores and databases (e.g. Oracle DBMS, Mongo DB, etc.)

4   Conclusions

Modern enterprise IT architecture needs to reflect current trends and support cloud deployment of applications, enable mobile computing and integration with IoT devices. This

allows application developers to focus on the functionality that directly supports business processes and adds value for the end users. The requirements for such a framework include a single sign-on and user authentication regardless of the physical location of the user, support for different devices such as mobile phones, tablets, notebooks, but also for IoT devices, and the ability to deploy applications on different cloud platforms in a secure and effective manner (i.e. minimizing the cost and maximizing performance). The main contribution of this paper is the description of the Unicorn Application Framework (UAF), a recently introduced framework for the development of enterprise applications at Unicorn that addresses the above requirements, and is expected to improve application development productivity, and at the same time minimize the risk of project failures.

5   References

[1]   Blair, G.S., et al., "An architecture for next generation middleware," in *Proceedings of the IFIP International Conference on Distributed Systems Platforms and Open Distributed Processing*. Springer-Verlag, 1998, p. 191-206.

[2]   Corba, O., *Common object request broker architecture*. Vol. 2. 1995.

[3]   Horstmann, M. and M. Kirtland., *DCOM architecture*. Microsoft white paper, 1997.

[4]   Platt, D.S., *Introducing Microsoft. Net*. Microsoft press, 2002.

[5]   Sun Microsystem. (2007) Java EE at a Glance. [Online]. Available: http://java.sun.com/javaee/

[6]   Pautasso, C., O. Zimmermann, and F. Leymann, "Restful web services vs. big web services: making the right architectural decision," in *Proceedings of the 17th*

international conference on World Wide Web. ACM, 2008.

[7]   Mahmood, Z. and S. Saeed, *Software engineering frameworks for the cloud computing paradigm.* Springer, 2013.

[8]   Raj, P., V. Venkatesh, and R. Amirtharajan, "Envisioning the cloud-induced transformations in the software engineering discipline", in *Software Engineering Frameworks for the Cloud Computing Paradigm.* Springer, 2013, p. 25-53.

[9]   Krishna, R. and R. Jayakrishnan, "Impact of cloud services on software development life cycle," in *Software Engineering Frameworks for the Cloud Computing Paradigm*, Springer, 2013, p. 79-99.

[10] Feuerlicht, G. and H.T. Tran, "Adapting service development life cycle for cloud," in *17th International Conference on Enterprise Information Systems*, Spain, Barcelona, Scitepress, 2015.

[11] Feuerlicht, G. and H.T. Tran, "Service consumer framework: Managing Service Evolution from a Consumer Perspective," in *16th International Conference on Enterprise Information Systems*, Portugal, Springer, 2014.

[12] Ramachandran, M., "Business requirements engineering for developing cloud computing services," in *Software Engineering Frameworks for the Cloud Computing Paradigm*, Springer, 2013, p. 123-143.

ISBN: 1-60132-458-8, CSREA Press ©

A Rapid Auto-Scaling Mechanism in Cloud Computing Environment

Chia-Wei Tseng, Ming-Shiun Tsai, Yao-Tsung Yang, Li-Der Chou

Dept. of Computer Science and Information Engineering, National Central, Taoyuan, Taiwan

Abstract - *With the rapid development of the Internet, Cloud Technology has been the most valued and praised solution for the purpose of reducing network service operating costs and increasing service efficiency. Virtualization technologies are the core of cloud computing. In the past few years container-based virtualization got mature and especially Docker gained a lot attention. Docker provides an ideal environment for deployment of services with regards to speed and operating cost. In this paper, we design and implement an integrated virtualization cloud platform that enables the quick and easy deployment of Virtual Network Functions (VNFs). In order to achieve lightweight and flexibly network services, this paper propose a Fuzzy-based Real-time Auto-Scaling (FARS) mechanism to provide a dynamic and real-time Automatic Scaling of Internet Applications in Cloud environment.*

Keywords: Auto-Scaling, NFV, VNF, Cloud Computing, Network Management

1   Introduction

Cloud computing is a model for enabling convenient, on-demand network access to a shared pool of configurable computing resources (e.g., networks, servers, storage, applications, and services) that can be rapidly provisioned and released with minimal management effort or service provider interaction. This cloud model promotes availability and is composed of five essential characteristics (On-demand self-service, Broad network access, Resource pooling, Rapid elasticity, Measured Service); three service models (Cloud Software as a Service (SaaS), Cloud Platform as a Service (PaaS), Cloud Infrastructure as a Service (IaaS)); and, four deployment models (Private cloud, Community cloud, Public cloud, Hybrid cloud) [1]. Virtualization technology is the key of cloud computing development; only with the supports of virtualization technologies can the underlying hardware resources be integrated for cloud computer to use. Since the fact that the popular virtualization technologies of Hypervisor failed to satisfy the demands of resource flexibility required by developers and Cloud Service Providers (CSPs), the more lightweight virtualization technology--Container was further developed. In terms of mass and rapid deployment, container boasts same and even better performance both in efficiency and flexibility compared with Virtual Machine (VM) based virtualization technologies. However, due to the technological

traits of container, the applications must share the same operational system resource, which may result in some security concerns.

In the cloud computer network, it spends more operating costs when adopting static resource configurations to maintain quality of service (QoS). In consequence, the Auto-Scaling technologies capable of adjusting service resources in a dynamic manner based on number of service demands. Auto-Scaling technology is able to maintain the high availability of services, which can automatically deployment more service resources in the peak of service demands; on the contrary, it can reduce service resources in the off-peak period of service demands to reduce the service operating costs. Most of the CSPs and virtualization components, such as Amazon Web Service CloudWatch, Microsoft Azure Schedule Scaling, VMware vCloud and OpenStack in the markets are all VM based Auto-Scaling solutions. In addition, many Auto-Scaling policies have been proposed in the past decade to decide on behalf of cloud customers when and how to provision resources to a cloud application utilizing cloud elasticity features [2][3][4]. And their algorithms are Prospective or Event-Driven Reactive methods. The Prospective Reactive mode, however, requires machine learning costs and fails to respond to the results when there are emergency demands from users; although Event-Driven Reactive mode is able to respond to the emergency service demands, but it still fails to make effective and proper response when the demands of users change rapidly.

This research mainly refers to the structure proposed in NFV Architectural Framework by ETSI NFV ISG and switches to apply integrated virtualization technologies. To solve the Auto-Scaling of data center, this paper also designs a Fuzzy-based Real-time Auto-Scaling mechanism based on the characteristics of the container-based virtualization technology. The main contributions of this paper are (i) designs and implements an integrated virtualization cloud platform and (ii) proposes a rapid Auto-Scaling mechanism to automatically scale up the computing resource based on workload information and performance desire.

The rest of the paper is organized as follows: in Section II, the background and related works are addressed. Section III describe the design of Integrated-Virtualization Cloud

ISBN: 1-60132-458-8, CSREA Press ©

platform and the proposed FRAS mechanism. The last section concludes this paper.

2 Background and Related Works

Virtualization techniques are widely used in enterprises over the last few years. System virtualization is most commonly implemented with hypervisor technology. There are two types of hypervisor: a bare-metal hypervisor, also known as Type 1 (e.g. Xen and EXSi); or a hosted hypervisor, also known as Type 2 (e.g. VMware Workstation and Oracle VirtualBox). There are important differences between a hosted and bare-metal virtualization hypervisor, and each has pretty specific use cases [5]. Container technology is different from that of hypervisor in Hardware Abstraction Layers for virtualization [6]. Container is a kind of virtualization technology at Operating System Level, the biggest difference between container and hypervisor lies in Kernel, a sharing operating system. Container technology is based on Linux Container (LXC), which assign the hardware resources of different software by namespace of original operating system and shared API. Linux container can be regarded as a storage for storing VNF image and the storage can be private or public available on the internet, such as Docker Hub[7]. In order to deploy VNF in a rapid manner, the Linux container is designed in layered and stacked manner. The advanced multi layered unification filesystem (AUFS) at the bottom is applied which stacks up many different VNF images. Container leverages AUFS technology to enable image sharing and minimize the use of disk space. Linux containers run on a single computing instance, making it easier to detect their activity and retire unused containers. Therefore, the utilization of CPU, memory efficiency, and the basic requirements of storage space can be considerably reduced. In view of the above mentioned, Container is recognized as a lightweight virtualization solution. The present cloud entrepreneurs of container, Google and Amazon, are engaged in integrating container and VM technologies. There are two reasons for integrating these two virtualization technologies, the first is the security aspect of container requires better isolation. The second is that applications need process resource management, network planning, security and storage when they are operated either in VM or Container and there have already had complete solutions for these technologies on VM platform. However, the solutions on container are relatively not well-established [8].

3 Integrated Virtualized Cloud Platform

The integrated virtualization cloud platform structure designed in this paper is based on Rancher [9]. The system architecture of the proposed IV cloud platform is shown in Figure 1. All of basic service units on integrated virtualization cloud platform are based on container. Among which the core Orchestrator is built by a Docker container and Orchestrator is connected with external network and controls all Docker Engine under the system via Bridge. Management Agent will collect the container, virtual machine information, etc. from the virtual host, and then converge and convert them to the

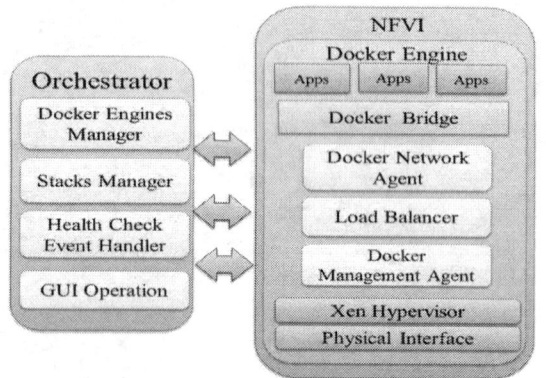

Figure 1 Integrated Virtualization Cloud Platform System Architecture

orchestrator. Unlike the structure proposed by ETSI, this Agent structure is beneficial for considerably reducing the burden of orchestrator, especially for decreasing orchestrator connections required to be built when there are mass deployments. Apart from Docker Management Agent, Docker Engine will also deploy a Network Agent which is responsible for managing all network functions in the system. The Network Agent will create corresponding VPN encrypted tunnels according to requirements, the same stack group container can exchange data over a private network even on different physical devices. No additional network configuration effort is required. In order to realize the Load Balancing function, the system also offer a Load Balancing functional module which can forward users' service demands to the Stack Manager. When there are timeout events, Docker Management Agent will return the data to health Check Event Handler on Orchestrator. Orchestrator will generate new Load Balancing configure file and send back to the Docker Management Agent when receiving VNF events. The Docker Management Agent will then apply the Load Balancing module to the configure file to the Load Balancing module for the purpose of load balancing. Orchestrator is the most important part. The Orchestrator-Agent structure is adopted in the system. Unlike other NFV systems, all resource monitoring on NFV infrastructure, VNF deployment and health check are done by Docker Management Agent. The data will be uniformly integrated for orchestrator to record and make decisions, whereas, all orchestrator decisions are made by agent demands. This hierarchical management structure is capable of significantly reducing orchestrator management overhead which is more suitable for mass-deployed container platforms. It's very important, to collect information with resource utilization since Orchestrator needs to allocate the resources and status of the entire platform. The resource status of each VNF needs to be monitored when the service is running online.

In order to achieve lightweight and flexibly network services, a rapid Auto-Scaling mechanism is built-in the integrated virtualization cloud platform. Auto-Scaling mechanism is an application with high availability, by this mechanism, the system is capable of adjusting the number of VNF deployment in dynamic manner based on users' demands and system performance status. As shown in Figure 2, when

ISBN: 1-60132-458-8, CSREA Press ©

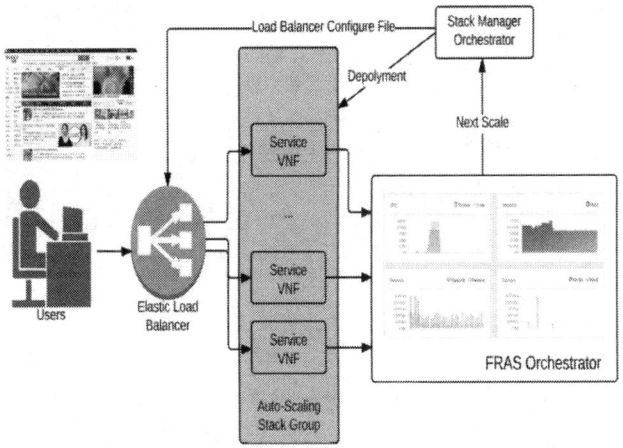

Figure 2 Auto-Scaling mechanism operation diagram

IF cpu is HIGH,	mem is HIGH and net is HIGH,	THEN scale HIGH
IF cpu is HIGH,		THEN scale HIGH
IF cpu is MEDIUM,		THEN scale MEDIUM
IF cpu is MEDIUM, mem is HIGH and net is MEDIUM,		THEN scale MEDIUM
IF cpu is MEDIUM, mem is LOW and net is LOW,		THEN scale MEDIUM
IF cpu is MEDIUM, mem is LOW and net is MEDIUM,		THEN scale MEDIUM
IF cpu is LOW	and net is MEDIUM,	THEN scale LOW
IF cpu is LOW,		THEN scale LOW
IF cpu is LOW,	and net is LOW,	THEN scale LOW
IF cpu is MEDIUM and mem is LOW,		THEN scale LOW

Figure 3 Fuzzy Logical rules

there are VNF timeouts, users will send service requests to Load Balancer, such as HTTP Request, and the service request will be imported into Stack Group by Load Balancer. More than one VNF in Stack Group is responsible for the service request of users. VNF must submit system status information to Orchestrator which will calculate next VNF deployment number with FRAS algorithm and send it back to Stack Manager. And finally, Stack Manager will deploy VNF and update the configure file of Load Balancer.

Because the resource utilization in cloud network is rapidly changing, it is hard to make decisions and manage with accurate judgement. Therefore, this paper adopts Fuzzy-based theory making Orchestrator carry out more accurate resource distribution. The membership function of each input value should first be defined before entering Fuzzy processes. In this study, Gaussian distribution is used to define membership function. Analysis which picks the monitored data of CPU, Disk and Memory to predict the resource utilization of the next time period. For example, calculations of CPU shown as equations (1), (2) and, (3). P_{CPU} means the average CPU load as the input of Fuzzy logic control. $\mu_{cpu,h}$, $\mu_{cpu,h}$, and $\mu_{cpu,h}$ are Gaussian distribution to the membership function of P_{CPU}. $\sigma_{cpu,h}$, $\sigma_{cpu,h}$ and $\sigma_{cpu,h}$ are the standard deviation of Gaussian distribution to the membership function of P_{CPU}.

After Fuzzy processes, these parameters will be translated into operable grade of membership based on fuzzy logic. In the next stage, Fuzzy Inference will be adopted. The Fuzzy Inference here must be deduced based on logical rules in Fuzzy Database shown in Figure 3, the Fuzzy rules deduced will take formula (4). R refers to the Fuzzy rules of deduced database and A_i^l & B^l means the Fuzzy set. Fuzzy Inference will take Minimum Inference Mechanism, such as formula (5) to measure the impacts all grade of membership exerting on final results for the next deployment scale.

$$R^l: IF\ x\ is\ A_i^l\ THEN\ y\ is\ B^l \tag{4}$$

$$\mu_{scale}(y) = \max_{1<l<m} \left[A_1^l(x_1) \cdot A_2^l(x_2) \cdot B^l(y) \right] \tag{5}$$

4 Experiment Results

The experiment will use JMeter [10] to simulate a large amount of user access to the system. The experiment environment is shown in Figure 4. Table 1 shows the experiment parameters. The DC/OS Auto-scaling Marathon services[3] and C-Scale[4] are compared with the proposed FRAS protocol. Figure 5 shows the experiment result, the X-axis refers to testing time, Y main axis refers to the scale size of the service, namely, the number of VNF enabled; Y subsidiary axis refers to service request rate. Orange dotted line is the pressure test reference.

$$\mu_{cpu,h}(P_{CPU}) = exp\left[-\frac{(x - \mu_{cpu,h})^2}{2\delta_{cpu,h^2}} \right] \tag{1}$$

$$\mu_{cpu,m}(P_{CPU}) = exp\left[-\frac{(x - \mu_{cpu,m})^2}{2\delta_{cpu,m^2}} \right] \tag{2}$$

$$\mu_{cpu,l}(P_{CPU}) = exp\left[-\frac{(x - \mu_{cpu,l})^2}{2\delta_{cpu,l^2}} \right] \tag{3}$$

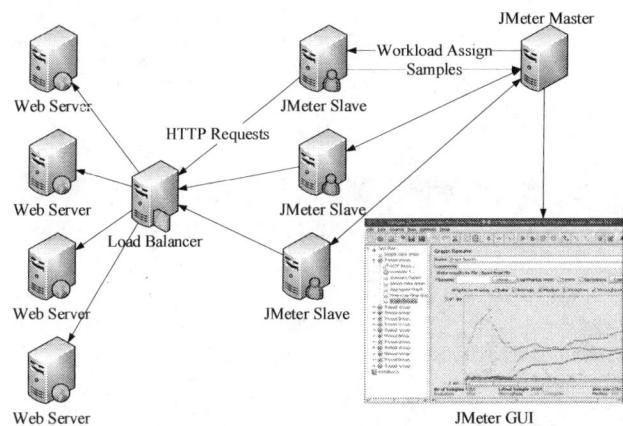

Figure 4 Experiment Environment

ISBN: 1-60132-458-8, CSREA Press ©

Table 1 Experiment Parameters

Parameter Name	Value
Number of initial instances	1 VNF
Experiment Time	8000 sec
Request Constant Throughput Time	600 sec
Max instances	24 VNFs
Auto-Scaling Period Time	90 sec
Number of Resource Measures	40
Number of Samples per second	100
Max HTTP Request Rate	7000 hits/sec

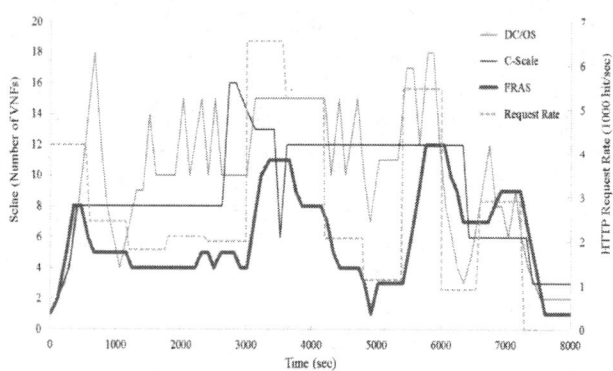

Figure 5 Experiment result

DC/OS mechanism is used to observe the CPU or memory threshold, and when either of the utilization of these two resources is over or under a threshold, the scale size of next scale period will be measured based on existing scale size. As shown in Figure 5, although the exponential growth adopted by Auto-Scaling mechanism of DC/OS is able to realize the expected service scale in short time, at the time around 2000 seconds, we can see that system scale keeps changing between 15 and 10. This unsteadiness situation is caused by the DC/OS scale mechanism changes too much. C-Scale is a multiplying exponentially Auto-Scaling algorithm which takes more time to scale up. In addition, the C-Scale's release resources threshold is relatively high, so it's expected to avoid scale down under the circumstance of sufficient resources. This method is effective in reducing error and delay, but it still adds a lot of unnecessary deployment costs. Compared with other mechanisms, the proposed FRAS mechanism meets pressure service requests best. The Fuzzy approaches work as an automatic decision making so that FRAS can adjustment resource accordingly.

5   Conclusions

This paper designs and implements an integrated virtualization cloud platform. The Hypervisor and Container-based virtualization technologies are integrated in the proposed cloud platform. The FARS mechanism built-in the integrated virtualization cloud platform is addressed to achieve lightweight and flexibly network services. According to experiment results, the Auto-Scaling strategy adopted by FRAS makes a quicker response to rapidly-changing service demand pressures. Besides, Fuzzy-based mechanism can accurately reflect the service resource state of the system on the deployment scaling.

6   Acknowledgment

The work described in this paper was supported by Ministry of Science and Technology of the Republic of China. (Project No. 104-2221-E-008-039-MY3 and 105-2221-E-008-071-MY3)

7   References

[1] NIST, SP 800-145, The NIST Definition of Cloud Computing [Online] Available: http://dx.doi.org/10.6028/NIST.SP.800-145

[2] Amazon Web Services Inc., 'AWS | Auto Scaling - Amazon Web Services", 2016. [Online] https://aws.amazon.com/autoscaling/.

[3] Mesosphere. "Autoscaling Marathon services", 2016. [Online] https://docs.mesosphere.com/1.7/usage/tutorials/autoscaling/cpu-memory/.

[4] C. Jin-Lin. "Implement an NFV system in OpenStack", Master Thesis, Institute of Network Engineering College of Computer Science, National Chiao Tung University, 2016

[5] Hagen Lauer and Nicolai Kuntze. "Hypervisor-Based Attestation of Virtual Environments", 2016 Intl IEEE Conferences on Ubiquitous Intelligence & Computing, Advanced and Trusted Computing, Scalable Computing and Communications, Cloud and Big Data Computing, Internet of People, and Smart World Congress, pp.333-340, 2016.

[6] Container and Hypervisor Structure, [Online] https://www.docker.com/what-docker

[7] Docker Hub, [Online] https://hub.docker.com/

[8] Andrea Tosatto, Pietro Ruiu and Antonio Attanasio. "Container-Based Orchestration in Cloud: State of the Art and Challenges", 2015 Ninth International Conference on Complex, Intelligent, and Software Intensive Systems, pp.70-75, 2015

[9] Rancher. [Online] http://rancher.com/

[10] Jmeter. [Oneline] http://jmeter.apache.org/

EZPoll: a Progressive Implementation of Cloud-Based Polling Systems

Hans Dulimarta

School of Computing and Information Systems, Grand Valley State University, Allendale, Michigan, USA

Abstract—*Many studies have shown that incorporating active learning in classroom improves the overall learning outcomes. Instructors are faced with many different options for incorporating active learning into their classroom, among these options is technology-enhanced learning. This paper focuses on electronic polling systems as an enhancement to classroom teaching/learning environment. More specifically, it discusses design requirements for cloud-based polling systems and explores several frameworks for implementing such a system. Using EZPoll as a case study, the paper presents several modern web frameworks and describes how they are selected and incorporated into EZPoll implementation. In addition, it also describes the challenges encountered with incorporating each framework and how we sought alternative solutions.*

Keywords: active learning, technology-enhanced learning, electronic voting systems, cloud-based voting systems

1. Introduction

Active learning provides instructors with an alternative to traditional classroom settings where students passively listen to lecture and occasionally ask questions to the instructor. To incorporate active learning in classroom, instructors are required to design in-class activities that encourage students to perform individual or group work, reflect upon the current topic of discussion, or any other activities that allow the instructor to immediately assess how well the students have learned the materials.

Michael lists several approaches for incorporating active learning[1]:

- Problem-based or case-based learning
- Cooperative/collaborative learning/group work of all kinds
- Think-pair-share or peer instruction
- Conceptual change strategies
- Inquiry-based learning
- Discovery learning
- Technology-enhanced learning

Instructors who teach a class that has an associated lab session may claim that their students participate in active learning in the lab. Laboratory assignments can be designed to require students use additional resources not practical to use in classroom.

This paper focuses on technology-enhanced learning, therefore we will investigate this approach in more details. Some examples of technology-enhanced learning that can be used in a lab environment are:

- In a physics lab, students use a simulation software to enforce their understanding of Newton's law of gravity
- In a language lab, students use a digital audio system to listen to phrases in a foreign language, record themselves repeating the phrases, compare and analyze their progress while learning the foreign language

The teacher's claim about their students' active learning in lab is true, but the main focus of active learning is to also keep students more engaged during lecture sessions.

Freeman *et al.* [2] performed a metaanalysis on 225 studies on using active learning in the STEM field and concluded that active learning improves the overall STEM classroom performance. One of their results shows that the average failure rate in traditional STEM classes is 33.8%, while the failure rate for STEM classes that incorporate active learning drops to 21.8%.

The short list of examples shown above seem to require hefty additional resources provided by the host institution before teachers can incorporate technology-based active learning. A low-cost alternative to incorporating active learning in a classroom is to use audience response systems (ARS) [4], [5]. Other acronyms have actually been used to label such systems: Electronic Voting Systems, Interactive Voting Systems, Classroom Assessment Systems, Personal Response Systems, Student Response System, and many other names [6], [7]. In the context of this article, we will be using Interactive Voting Systems (IVS) to refer to such systems.

Interactive Voting Systems are becoming easier to incorporate and are used by secondary schools and college educators [3]. The hardware requirements to use IVS in classroom has evolved from a dedicated hardware to practically "none". The initial inception of IVS requires each student use a special remote (similar to remotes for typical home Audio Visual system) for sending responses to a dedicated receiver installed by the instructor in classroom. The more recent IVSs require no dedicated hardware used by either the student or the instructor, student responses are delivered to a cloud-based polling system using their smartphones.

Based on a review of 67 peer-reviewed papers related to use of IVSs in classroom, Kay and LeSage present the benefits and challenges associated with the use of IVSs [8]. They further classified the benefits under several categories: classroom environment benefits, learning benefits, and assessment benefits. The classroom environment benefits include: increased attendance, higher student attention, student anonymity, and engagement. The learning benefits include: positive interaction, more discussions, contingent teaching, improved learning performance. The assessment benefits include: immediate feedback and ability to compare responses with peers.

Besides the benefits, Kay and LeSage also identify several challenges:

- Technological challenges: students do not bring remote to class and technical hardware problems (unable to connect remote)
- Teacher-centered challenges: preparing excellent questions, responding to student feedback,
- Student-centered challenges: using a new method of learning, fear of being monitored

The rest of this paper is organized as follow. In Section 2 we describe a general architecture of cloud-based polling systems. Section 3 describes EZPoll, a system used in our case study. Section 4 shows the current state of EZPoll and how to use it. Finally, we conclude and describe our future plans in Section 5.

2. Cloud-Based Polling Systems

Our current students are part of the millenial generation. They carry a smartphone everywhere they go and are connected to their digital space all the time. They practically know how to carry out most tasks using their phone. Therefore, connecting to a cloud service to participate in an online poll is a task that does not require further instructions for them. This is one of the reasons, why cloud-based polling systems such as: PollEverywhere, TopHat, Kahoot are becoming very popular.

2.1 Design Requirements

For a classroom setting, the two main groups of users of a cloud-based polling system are students and instructors. Basic features provided by a cloud-based polling system should be designed around common core tasks performed by these two user groups:

- *Concurrent Multi-User Support*: the first and the most important requirement is ability to handle concurrent operations performed by many users connected to the system.
- *Content Preparation*: Prior to in-class delivery of quiz/survey questions, instructors must prepare these questions based on a particular topic. A web-based polling environment should allow instructors to login, create and edit questions, and save them for later use in classroom. To mitigate one of the teachers' challenges

in preparing excellent questions as Kay and LeSage identified above, the system can provide a feature for instructors to *share* their questions.

- *Audience Participation*: When an instructor is ready to begin a quiz/survey session, the system should allow him to create a publicly available web address for the students to participate in the session. For easy on-boarding, students should be allowed to participate either anonymously in addition to using a verified account.
- *Poll Delivery*: Instantaneous content delivery is a necessary feature for any cloud-based polling systems. In such systems, data flow in two directions. The downstream flow delivers content from the cloud to the user devices and the upstream flow transmits user responses.
- *Post Analysis*: after participating in an online classroom quiz, students may be interested in getting feedback on their performance in the quiz. Likewise, instructors may want to review which topics are well- and poorly-understood by students, so she can make necessary changes to improve the lecture.

In addition to the above core tasks, provision of the following features will increase user productivity in using the system:

- Allow instructors to create "problem sets" from a list of available questions
- Import/Export question database (between the cloud-based server and the local computer)
- Automatic attendance taking
- Allow students/participants to ask questions electronically
- Allow students to delete their account. Student will be using the system only while they are in school. After graduation, they will not be using the system anymore.

2.1.1 Content Delivery

Between the two data streams mentioned above, the upstream data connections are easier to implement. Each client sends unicast requests to the server. The server views these connections just like any other web requests. On the contrary, downstream delivery requires more advanced techniques. There are two main techniques for the downstream content delivery:

- Pull: the audience device must continuously monitor for updated contents initiated by the server. This technique is easier to implement, but it is not a viable option if the client remote device is a power-constrained smartphone.
- Push: the application server multicasts contents to all the client devices. To prevent updates being delivered to an unauthorized target device, this technique requires client device registration so both the server and the client agree on a common authentication token.

ISBN: 1-60132-458-8, CSREA Press ©

The "third" option is a combination of both pull and push techniques. Using this hybrid approach, the server initiates a push by sending an initial message that contains only a portion of the intended payload, just a necessary piece of information required for the client to pull the complete content from the server. This hybrid technique has a potential to offer lower data traffic: only the clients interested in the detailed contents proceed to the next step of pulling it. Other clients may ignore the contents embedded in the initial push.

Among the pioneers of the push technology are Apple and Google. Both Apple Push Notifications (APN) and Google Cloud to Device Messaging (GC2DM) are initially targeted for server to mobile device content delivery. GC2DM was rebranded to Google Cloud Message (GCM) and rebranded again to Firebase Cloud Messaging.

2.2 Implementation of Cloud-Based Polling Systems

To address the design requirements mentioned above, a cloud-based polling system should incorporate the following components:

- Persistent storage for instructors to save their quiz/survey questions, post polling analysis, student performance
- Instructor's front-end that includes a dashboard organized into different sections for instructors to perform their core tasks (authoring questions, content delivery, analysis, etc.)
- Student's front-end, a much simpler interface than the instructor's dashboard to allow a student responds to posted questions, review his/her progress, and personalized settings.
- A real-time message delivery infrastructure for handling both upstream and downstream traffic described above.
- Authentication system to manage user accounts

There are many technological choices for implementing a cloud-based polling system that incorporates the above components. For instance, Amazon Web Services provides offer products like: Amazon RDS, Amazon Aurora, DynamoDB, and many other. Google Cloud Storage offers products like: Cloud Storage, Datastore, Cloud SQL, Firebase, Cloud Spanner, etc.

The options for implementation the user interface are as overwhelmingly long as the available choices of cloud storage products, some example of modern web frameworks are: Angular, Meteor, Poymer, React, and Ember.

In the next section, we describe EZPoll, the system implemented for our case study.

3. EZPoll

EZPoll is a cloud-based polling system designed for classroom use. A typical EZPoll session would require an instructor to login via a web-browser and initiates a polling session. Students in the classroom participate in the session using either a smartphone (Android or iOS) or a web browser. Using a web client front-end, the instructor can multicast selected questions to all the students in the classroom.

In the following sections we will describe EZPoll implementation and its evolution as various web platforms were incorporated into its implementation. We begin with our initial approach building it on the Google AppEngine.

3.1 Google App Engine

As one of the services of the Google Cloud platform, AppEngine provides developers a cloud infrastructure to run their server logic. The broad support for many programming languages enables developers to choose a language that best fits their application design. Currently, AppEngine supports Java, Go, PHP, Python, Node, .NET, and Ruby. Application data can be stored using one of the available options: relational DBs, scalable storage, and lightweight storage.

Our initial design calls for a web front-end used by instructors and an Android client for students. To mitigate code maintenance chaos, we decided to implement EZPoll application server in Java, the same implementation language for developing the associated Android client. The web front-end was built using JavaScript and jQuery. The downstream data from the application server to the Android clients was implemented using Google Cloud Messaging (GC2DM).

Our choice of using Google AppEngine calls for designing our own back-end APIs that will be invoked by the Android client. The typical development cycle dictated by our design choice had to follow these steps:

1) Develop the datastore classes (with Java Data Objects annotations). Each of these classes represents a "record" in the datastore
2) Develop the backend (endpoint) classes in Java. These classes work in conjuction with the datastore class in the previous step and it defines the API methods to manipulate the datastore.
3) Enhance the backend classes with necessary Java annotations needed by the client library generator (next step below)
4) Generate the custom client libraries (to be included by either the Android client code or web client in JavaScript)
5) Develop the rest of the Android classes and JavaScript code

The above steps are required because essentially we were developing three interrelated components:

- The web APIs for accessing the datastore
- The web client logic (for instructor's front-end)
- The android client logic (for student's front-end)

The AppEngine related classes required to support EZPoll basic operations are shown in Table 1.

ISBN: 1-60132-458-8, CSREA Press ©

Table 1: EZPoll Model Classes

Class	Description
DeviceInfo	device registration token and current session
MessageData	downstream messages
PollResponse	response submitted by students
Question	quiz/survey question
Session	polling session

The following code snippet show an ApiMethod annotation for an API method to search a question with a specific id.

```
@ApiMethod (name = "getQuestion")
public Question getQuestion(@Named("id") String id) {
    EntitiyManager mgr = getEntityManager();
    Question q = mgr.find (Question.class, id);
    return q;
}
```

Push notifications via Google Cloud Messaging require participation of the following three parties:

- The application server that creates a message to deliver
- The GCM server that delivers the message
- The client as the recipient of the message

To receive push notifications from the instructor's web app, each Android client must first register itself with the GCM server. Upon a successful registration, the Android client receives a unique registration ID that must be used by the application server when sending a message to the client.

To push a content payload, the application server must cooperates with the GCM server. All messages pushed from the application server have to go through the GCM server. Developers who opt for this approach must design their system for the following two-step initialization:

1) Establish a connection between their application server and the GCM server. This connection is required for sending multicast messages to all registered devices.
2) Configure the client app to register itself with the GCM server and sends its registration ID to the application server.

3.2 AppEngine Channel API

GCM provides a solution for delivering contents to mobile devices. In our case, this feature is needed for multicasting questions to students' devices. Besides that, our application server also needs to send unicast messages to the web client front-end. The communication channel for these messages is implemented using the AppEngine Channel API.

3.3 Polymer

Implementing an attractive UI using only HTML and CSS is a tedious task. With jQuery used in our initial implementation, the most natural upgrade path is to incorporate jQuery-UI or a similar framework such as Bootstrap. However, we are interested in using the web components technology in our implementation. Hence our decision of adopting Polymer [9]

for desiging EZPoll web user interface. As an early adopter of Polymer, we began with with redesigning the instructor's front-end using Polymer 0.5 components. We later migrated to Polymer 0.8 and 1.0. A snippet of a web component used in our application is shown below[1]:

```
<polymer-element name="session-manager">
  <template>
    <paper-button on-click="{{exitSession}}"
                  label="Exit Session">
    </paper-button>
    <!-- other components here -->
  </template>
  <script>
  Polymer('session-manager', {
    /* other functions here */

    exitSession: function(event, detail, sender) {
      /* code for handling button click event */
    }
  });
  </script>
</polymer-element>
```

A Polymer custom element conveniently defines the UI layout and its handling logic within one file. All the UI elements making up a custom element are defined in the `<template>` section, while the corresponding JavaScript code for handling UI events or UI updates defined in the `<script>` section. In our case, the application server APIs associated with the AppEngine endpoints are invoked from the `<script>`.

Some of the Polymer custom elements developed in our application are coupled with the model classes we developed for the AppEngine application server. Table 2 shows a selected sample of these elements.

Table 2: Polymer Custom Elements and AppEngine Model Classes

Custom Element	Description
<device-list>	user device
<question-manager>	quiz/survey question
<session-manager>	polling session

3.4 Polymer Data Binding

In designing our application using custom elements, we approach them like Android fragments. A fragment has its own lifecycle and manages a portion of the UI front-end. Likewise, a Polymer custom element has a predefined lifecycle function callbacks dictated by the Polymer framework (`create`, `ready`, `attached`, etc.).

To pass data into an Android fragment, the hosting activity invokes the fragment `setArguments()` method. Polymer uses a totally different technique, it employs data binding mechanism to pass data among custom elements. Specifically, Polymer allows one-way and two-way data binding:

---

[1]The snippet is shown using Polymer 0.5 syntax.
Our current implementation used Polymer 1.x

ISBN: 1-60132-458-8, CSREA Press ©

- In one-way binding (using the double square brackets syntax: `[[property]]`), data are passed from the host to the target element. Changes made to the property by the target element are not passed to the host.
- In two-way binding (using the double curly braces syntax: `{{property}}`), data are initially passed from the host to the target element and changes to the property are also observed by the host.

Polymer allows these two data binding notations be used together with other attributes (`readOnly` and `notify`) for a finer control of both *host-to-target* and *target-to-host* updates.

In the following snippet the properties `dsession` and `msession` are bound to the host variable `id`. Changes to `dsession` (by `device-list` does not propagate to `id` hence not observed by `msession`. On the contrary, changes to `msession` are propagated to `dsession` via the host property `id`.

```
<device-list dsession="[[id]]"></device-list>
<session-mgr msession="{{id}}"></session-mgr>
```

Using the analogy of parameter passing mechanisms, one-way to two-way binding is like *pass-by-value* to *pass-by-reference*. The ability to observe state changes in one element by another is required for the latter to respond accordingly. For instance, using the above example, when the session id of `<session-mgr>` becomes null, it can be used by `<device-list>` to notify all the connected device that the session just ended. However, we learned that two-way binding can create unexpected behaviors which are difficult to track down, especially when the binding is deeply nested with the DOM (Document Object Model) hierarchy. We were looking for an alternative approach to solve this problem, specifically we are looking for ways to eliminate (or minimize) two-way data binding.

3.5 Firebase

Our strategy of adopting incremental updates in our software development calls for frequent changes to the data model design, we tried several small updates and compared which one worked better. However, maintaining our own backend API to interface with AppEngine datastore hinders us from moving faster in reaching our goals. Minor changes in our data model forces us to regenerate the back end library for both our Android and web client. This hindrance motivated us to seek an alternative implementation for our datastore back end.

We had previous experience with Parse, but when we learned that Facebook was about to decommission Parse, we chose Firebase instead [11]. In addition, Firebase offers many options for user authentication, seamless migration for our use of cloud messaging, and most importantly we were relieved from back end maintenance tasks.

Our Firebase realtime database are organized into the following permanent three top-level JSON nodes:

- `authors`: a subtree that stores teachers' information
- `users`: a subtree that stores students' information
- `questions`: a subtree that stores all the questions created by teachers

In addition to the above permanent nodes, transient nodes for sessions are also created at runtime whenever a teacher initiates a polling session in classroom.

3.6 In Search of MVx

To promote use of unit testing into their software development cycle, mobile and web developers adopt the best practices in designing the architecture of their apps. Among the popular design architectures that have proven their success are Model-View-Controller (MVC), Model-View-Presenter (MVP), Model-View-ViewModel (MVVM), Model-View-ViewModel-Coordinator (MVVM-C), and so on. Certain frameworks dictate developers to use a particular architecture. For instance, iOS is tightly coupled with MVC. But, other frameworks allow developers to incorporate practically any design architecture for implementating their software.

To facilitate testing of EZPoll functionalities, we first attempted to incorporate the MVP pattern into EZPoll. Among the ideas for applying MVP is to to restructure a web app into the following components:

- Model, implemented by asynchronous REST calls
- View, implemented by DOM (Document Object Model)
- Presenter that handles UI events

The above proposed idea does not explicitly answer our problem of eliminating two-way data binding mentioned earlier. However, after watching a Polymer Summit 2016 presentation by Gray Norton [10], we were more motivated to redesign our app and thrive for "thinner" Polymer elements by factoring out application logic from the custom elements into our model objects. In the presentation, Norton also mentions that the technique he described works with third-party framework like Redux [14]. In addition, during our research for adopting MVx, we came across the Unidirectional Data Flow architecture [12] powered by Flux [15]. Between Redux and Flux, we decided to move forward with Redux.

In online forums, discussions on using the Redux/React combo are more popular than discussions on using Redux with Polymer. This is probably the natural consequence of the web developer community migrating their projects from using Flux/React to using Redux/React. Another logical reason is because both Redux and Polymer are relatively young projects (version 1.x of both projects were released around mid 2015). Fortunately, by the end of 2016 web developers who are trying to adopt Polymer and Redux saw a great hope when they learned about the Polymer-Redux project [13]. This library enables declarative data binding between Redux states and custom element properties.

3.7 Redux

The main core of Redux is a finite state machine that transforms and maintains your application states in one place. Changes to any one of the states can be observed by your application. Despite its ability to transform states, Redux imposes an additional constraint and states are *immutable* objects. To "transform" a state, you must create a new copy of the state and alter the copy. But the most important principle that fits our need is that Redux employs strict **unidirectional data flow**.

A Redux-based application must be designed to follow these principles [14]:

1) Single source of truth: the state of your whole application is stored in an object tree within a single store

2) State is read-only: the only way to change the state is to emit an action, an object describing what happened

3) Changes are made with pure functions: to specify how the state tree is transformed by actions, you write pure reducers.

The three principles also highlight the important role of these four components:

- State, the object tree that holds the application state
- Action, an object that describes the type of work to be done and additional data/payload needed to complete the work
- Reducers, maps the pair (oldstate, action) to (newstate), i.e. it uses the given action to transform the old state of the app to a new state
- A Store that hosts all the above components which are managed internally by Redux.

After incorporating Redux into EZpoll, our custom elements are much thinner. Most event handling functions in our Polymer custom elements are now a dispatcher to a reducer function. View updates to the custom elements are coupled directly to Redux observed state. For instance, Redux-related lines of our redesigned `ezpoll-login` custom element are shown in the following snippet:

```
<template>
  <paper-button on-tap="_onSignin">
    Sign In
  </paper-button>
  ...
  <span>Welcome [[user]]</span>
</template>
<script>
  Polymer ({
    is: 'ezpoll-login',
    behaviors: [ReduxBehavior],
    properties: {
      user: {
        type: String,
        statePath: 'user.email'
      }
    },

    _onSignin: function() {
      email = .....;
      passwd = .....;
```

```
      this.dispatch ('userSignin', email, passwd);
  }});
</script>
```

The on-tap handler function (`_onSignin`) calls the Redux dispatch() function to execute one of the action functions (userSignin) while passing the user's email and password (shown below). The `user` property is linked to Redux JavaScript object `user` containing an attribute `email`.

```
actions: {
  userSignin: function (eml, pwd) {
    return dispatch => {
      /* verify the credential */
      const userObj = authenticate (eml, pwd);
      dispatch ({type: 'SIGNIN_COMPLETED',
                 user: userObj});
  }}}
```

The `userSignin` function performs any required task such as verifying the given email and password before invoking Redux `dispatch` to trigger state updates. The `statePath` attribute attached to the `user` property causes the "Welcome" text in the view to be updated automatically.

After introducing Redux into our application, we are able to factor out application-related logic from all our Polymer custom elements. In addition, we also adopt another Redux best practice of partitioning our reducers into several smaller modules. Currently, EZpoll reducers are partitioned into the following:

- `loginReducer` is responsible for user login authentication, on-boarding, and other password management tasks.
- `authorReducer` handles instructor's core tasks other than in class online polling
- `sessionReducer` handles in-class online polling
- `voterReducer` handles students' core tasks

4. Current State of EZPoll

The current implementation of EZPoll is hosted on Firebase and is available at `https://ezpoll.io`. Any instructors interested in using it for classroom use must first create a new account with "Author Privilege" so they have the right permission to post questions to their audience. In addition, the "Author Privilege" allows them to create, save, and edit their own questions.

EZPoll is an on-going project with more new features continuously added and tested. As of this writing, it supports the following features:

- User on-boarding with email and password
- User on-boarding with author/teacher privilege
- Automated user account verification via email
- Anonymous/guest login
- Automated user password management (password reset)
- Polling session management: posting questions, deliver questions to connected users, show live polling results, etc.

ISBN: 1-60132-458-8, CSREA Press ©

- Students voting participation
- Create/Edit/Share questions by teachers

5. Conclusions and Future Work

This paper presents a case study of developing a cloud-based polling app using various web frameworks: Google AppEngine, jQuery, Polymer, Firebase, and Redux. We also describe challenges encountered in using each framework and how we address them by seeking alternative frameworks.

Among the immediate future work planned for the next major EZPoll updates are:

- Migrate all the custom elements to Polymer 2.0
- Incorporate RxJS into the web front-end
- Incorporate RxAndroid/RxJava framework into the companion Android, migrate the iOS clients to Swift 3 and incoporate RxSwift

References

[1] Joel Michael. (2006) "Where's the evidence that active learning works?" *Adv. Physiol. Education*, Vol 30, pp. 159–167.

[2] Scott Freeman, Sarah Eddy, Miles McDonough, Michelle Smith, Nndozie Okoroafor, Hannah Jordt, and Mary Wenderoth, "Active learning increases student performance in science, engineering, and mathematics", *Proceedings of the National Academy of Sciences of the United States of America*, Vol. 111, No. 23, June, 2014, pp. 8410–8415.

[3] Nathaniel Hunsu, Olusola Adesope, and Dan Bayly, "A meta-analysis of the effets of audience response systems (clicker-based tehcnologies) on cognition and affect, *Computers & Education*, Vol. 94, 2016, pp. 102–119.

[4] Harish Thampy and Zirva Ahmad, "How to use audience response systems", *Education for Primary Care*, Vol. 25, 2014, pp. 294–196.

[5] Lorena Blasco-Arcas, Isabel Buil, Blanca Hernández-Ortega, and F. Javier Sese, "Using clickers in class. The role of interactivity, active collaborative learning and engagement in learning performance", *Computers & Education*, Vol. 62, 2013, pp.102–110.

[6] Karen Moss and Mark Crowley, "Effective learning in science: the use of personal response systems with a wide range of audiences", *Computer & Education*, Vol. 56, 2011, pp. 36–43.

[7] Adam Wong and Simon Wong, "A cross-cohort exploratory study of student perceptions on mobile phone-based student response system using a polling website", *International Journal of Education and Development using Information and Communication Technology*, Vol. 12, 2016, pp. 58–78.

[8] Robin Kay and Ann LeSage, "Examining the benefits and challenges of using audience response systems: A review of the literature", *Computers & Education*, Vol. 53, 2009, pp. 819–827.

[9] (2017) The Polymer website. [Online]. Available: http://www.polymer-project.org/

[10] Gray Norton, "Data Flow in Polymer elements and apps", *Polymer Summit 2016*. [Online]. Available: https://www.youtube.com/watch?v=pAW4YDLtPVs

[11] (2017) The Firebase website. [Online]. Available: http://firebase.google.com

[12] Realm Cocoa Team, Building a Unidirectional Data Flow App in Swift with Realm, . [Online]. Available: https://realm.io/news/unidirectional-data-flow-in-swift/

[13] (2017) The Polyer Redux GitHub project. [Online]. Available: http://github.com/tur-nr/polymer-redux

[14] (2017) The Redux website. [Online]. Available: http://reduxjs.org

[15] (2017) The Flux website. [Online]. Available: http://facebook.github.io/flux

MCloud API For Managing Data in Multi-Cloud Environment

Maram Alhafdi [1], **Ahmed Barnawi**[1]

malhafzy0001@stu.kau.edu.sa, ambarnawi@kau.edu.sa

[1] Department of Information Technology, King Abdulaziz University, Jeddah, Saudi Arabia

Abstract - Cloud computing environment is one of the widely growing software deployment platforms in the world of technology. There is a continuous increase in using the cloud-based storage as service from developers and users. Cloud storage services provide numerous advantages such as high scalability, availability and pay-as-you-go cost model. In addition, cloud providers are offering different options for storage services. For example, Amazon provides S3 service as a scalable, durable and available distributed object store. Azure provides SQL databases as traditional SQL databases. In this domain, one of the biggest challenges is the interoperability between different storage systems from the various cloud providers, due to the lack of the unified methods for accessing, interfacing and managing the stored data. In this paper, we present our approach to address this challenge by building a system that enables the users and developers to manage their data hosted in different storage systems from the various cloud providers for a single point of interface. Our prototype is under evaluation.

Keywords: Cloud computing, data management, interoperability, vendor lock-in, multi-cloud, and storage systems.

1   Introduction

Cloud computing has become one of the hottest core technical topics in the modern software development era. The National Institute of Standards and Technology defined the cloud computing as "*a model for enabling convenient, resource pooling, ubiquitous, on-demand access which can be easily delivered with different types of service provider interaction*" [1]. Cloud storage is one of the most essential services of cloud computing, which offers storage-as-a-service that allows data owners to store their data in the cloud[2]. In practice, four different data storage and access mechanisms are common across the cloud vendor [3]:

- Blob storage also known as object storage is useful for storing unstructured data. Examples are Amazon S3 and IBM Cloud Object Storage.

- Table storage is non-relational databases called "NoSQL." An example of this is Amazon DynamoDB
- Queue storage is a dedicated queue storage mechanism, often used for fully managed message queuing service. For example, Amazon SQS
- Relational table storage is based on traditional SQL databases. For example, Amazon RDS, and Azure SQL databases

Different cloud providers such as Amazon, and Microsoft Azure, supported the previous storage systems and offered them to their customers. The user should use the front end or API to get access to or store the data. Unfortunately, those cloud providers incompatible with each other and created these services with different APIs. Therefore, the incompatibility in standards and formats while getting access to the cloud has become a big issue and causes vendor lock-in problem [4]. Consequently, one of the major challenges in cloud computing environment is cloud interoperability. Interoperability is defined as the ability of heterogeneous systems to work and interact together. For clouds, interoperability means the ability for multiple cloud providers to work together with minimal or null user effort. However, most of the cloud providers built their services without consideration of interoperability [5][6].

Some developers and users are more closely to use a particular storage type of a specific provider due to the features the provider is offering or the pricing of this service. For that, the user hosted his data on multi-cloud. When the user wants to access and manage his data, he will deal with different cloud interfaces and then he will face a problem in managing this hosted data due to vendor lock-in. Moreover, they face a lack of interoperability among these different cloud providers, and the unified methods for accessing, interfacing, and managing the stored data in these storage systems.

To address these challenges, we proposed building a unified interface (MCloud) to manage the data hosted in different storage systems in multi-cloud. MCloud standardizes APIs for Blob storage, Table storage, Queue storage, and Relational table storage, to allow developers and users to be independent from cloud vendors and to provide a transparent way for the users to access and manage their data. For Blob storage, MCloud supports Amazon Simple Storage Service (Amazon S3) and IBM Bluemix Object Storage. In addition, it supports DynamoDB for Table storage, and Amazon Simple Queue Service (SQS) for the Queue storage type. Finally, it supports Relational Database Service (RDS) from Amazon provider, and Azure SQL Database for Relational table storage.

The remainder of the paper is organized as follows. In the following section, we discuss the related work. In section 3, we explain the system design which we follow to implement MCloud. We present MCloud API, and the services it provides in section 4. In Section 5, we present the future work and conclusion.

2   Related Work

In the past, several researches about the unified cloud interfaces were published whether as independent ones or as a part of a broader approach. A majority of them focused on the infrastructure provisioning model [4], or the unified interfaces for application deployment and management among cloud platforms. Furthermore, existing approaches for PaaS focused on supporting a unified deployment of applications. In addition, the recent researches have focused more on the management capabilities for applications in the cloud such as developing, deploying and migrating multiple data stores. The following paragraphs provide an overview of the related work and demonstrate how our work differs and contributes to the existing approaches. Table 1 is a summary of related works and its limitations.

Several standardization organizations propose standards to overcome the vendor-in lock, and to deal with the data stored in a cloud environment. Storage Network Industry Association (SNIA) proposed Cloud Data Management Interface (CDMI), which is an ISO/IEC standard that enables cloud solution vendors to meet the growing need of interoperability for data stored in the cloud [7]. Open Cloud Computing Interface classified as a standardized approach for Open Cloud Computing Interface. It provides a set of specifications for cloud tasks such as deployment, dynamic scaling, and monitoring across different cloud providers. However, most standard proposals suffer from the lack of acceptance and participation by cloud providers [8].

Another approach to integrating multiple CSPs is to use proxy servers, which act as an intermediary among multiple CSPs providing transparent access, and gathering data from multiple CSPs, however, this approach is a single point of failure [9]. For example, CDMI-compatible proxy supports only two types of storage mentioned in section 1, blobs and queues storages [3]. Some applications like Cloudfuze, which is a centralized interface, are used to manage the files stored in different cloud service providers [10]. In addition, CYRUS [9] is a client-defined architecture that integrates multiple CSPs into one unified cloud and allows clients to share files and specify their desired performance levels. But these applications just support blob storage type.

SimpleCloud is an API that allows using the storage services independent of cloud platforms [8]. It is similar to our approach, but it allows the developers to write the portable code that can interoperate with multiple cloud vendors, however it only supports PHP language for web applications. MCloud provides a common interface to access and manage the hosted data in the multiple cloud providers, regardless of the programming language the developers use to build their applications. CDPort [6] proposed a common data model and a standardized API for NoSQL databases. Moreover, CDPort supported the transformation and exchange of data that is stored on NoSQL databases. It provided only NoSQL storage type.

Some researches focused on assisting the developers to manage their applications. Such as [11] which facilitates the developer's task and enables the development of applications using multiple data stores. The developer can use this approach to develop, deploy and migrate multiple data stores applications in cloud environments. A unified interface for application deployment and management among cloud platforms is presented in [4]. Openshift is a platform for developers to build, test, deploy and run cloud applications; it supports no-lock-in at PaaS level as approach in [4]. By using Openshift, the developer can focus only on designing and coding, whereas all the infrastructure and middleware management are handled by Openshift [8]. MCloud supports no-lock-in at SaaS level.

All these studies in the previous paragraph provide a way to assist the developers to manage their applications. Our research focused on supporting the developers to manage the data hosted in a cloud environment; it provides storage as a service to the developers. Therefore, a developer can access the storage from different cloud providers, provision it, view its details and manage it.

ISBN: 1-60132-458-8, CSREA Press ©

Table 1 — The Related works and its limitations

The aforementioned work	Limitations
Data Management Interface (CDMI)	Standards experience a lack of acceptance and participation by cloud providers
Open Cloud Computing Interface	
CDMI-compatible proxy	Do not support NoSQL storage and, Relational table storage
Cloudfuze	Only supports blob storage type
CYRUS	
SimpleCloud	Language dependent, only supports applications written in PHP language.
CDPort	It provides only NoSQL storage type.
Openshift	Supports no-lock-in at PaaS level

3   System Design

The aim of our interface is to unify the core management functions of the data hosted in multi-cloud. We focus solely on the creation of a management interface, which covers all storage types that mentioned in section 1. MCloud is using a layer for wrapping three SDKs of different clouds into a common API to get access to the data hosted in different storage systems as shown in Figure 1.

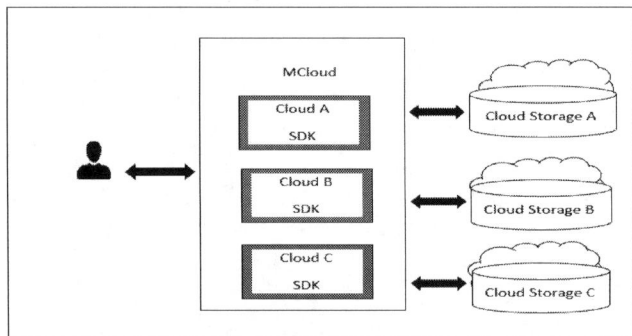

Figure 1— MCloud data access mechanisms

We define the following goals for our approach:
1. Standardize API system to allow the developers and users to be independent from the cloud vendors.
2. Provide a transparent way for the developers and users to manage their data that is stored in the different storage.

To achieve our goals, we built the interface with Python language using the SDKs for some cloud providers. Firstly, using Boto3 SDK provided by Amazon to enable MCloud to support four services: Amazon Simple Storage Service (s3), DynamoDB (NoSQL database), Relational Database Service (RDS), and Simple Queue Service (SQS). Secondly, using Azure SDK provided by Microsoft Azure to enable MCloud to support Azure SQL Database. Thirdly, using the Swiftclient SDK to enable the users to access the Object Storage service that is provided by IBM Bluemix.

MCloud is easy to install and setup, so it is useful to the end-user who cares about using blob storage from different cloud providers and needs a unified interface to manage his/her data. Furthermore, MCloud is helpful for the developer who cares about provision and uses a different storage system from various cloud providers.

4   MCloud API

MCloud is a common API for delivering different storage services over a multi-cloud. This platform supports all types of storage in cloud computing environment (blob storage, queue storage, table storage, and relational table storage). MCloud supports the interoperability among cloud providers in a transparent way, especially for the user who works with different storage systems from various cloud providers.

MCloud supports the four-different data storage and their services as the following:
1. Blob storage: MCloud supports two of the most common blob storage: Amazon Simple Storage Service (Amazon S3) and IBM Bluemix Object Storage. MCloud supported the operations of creating a bucket, emptying it, deleting it, and viewing its contents. It also facilitates the control over the bucket to upload files in it, download files from it, and delete files from it. Finally, the API also provides options to create and delete folders.

2. Table storage: MCloud facilitates the control over Amazon DynamoDB. API allows to create a table, delete it, and insert items in it. In addition, it supports the operations over items in the table; the user can update the item, delete it, and query it.

3. Queue storage: MCloud enables the user to get control over Amazon Simple Queue Service (SQS). Moreover, it supports delete queues, view queue details, purge queues, configure queues, and view the messages. In addition, it supports the operations of creating permissions, and deleting them. Finally,

the API also provides options for sending a message, and deleting it.

4. Relational table storage: MCloud supports two of the most common Relational table storages: Amazon Relational Database Service, and Azure SQL Database. MCloud facilitates control over these services. For Amazon(RDS), the user can create an instance, view its details, modify it, and delete it. For Azure SQL, API allows to create (SQL database, resource group, and server) and delete them. Finally, the API also provides options to view the databases on a server, view items of a resource group, and set server firewall.

5   Conclusion

As we mentioned, there are several solutions aiming to give transparent access to multiple storage systems. However, one solution cannot achieve all user requirements. There is still a problem in managing the data hosted in different storage services of various cloud providers. In addition, there is a lack of the unified methods for accessing, and managing this stored data. Therefore, we provide an approach to unify the interfaces for the storage services provided by various cloud providers. Our prototype is under evaluation. In future work, we aim to add more services which provide billing information about the storage the user used, and an approach for selecting the best storage type depending on the user requirements and the storage prices.

6   References

[1]   S. Singh, Y.-S. Jeong, and J. H. Park, "A survey on cloud computing security: Issues, threats, and solutions," *J. Netw. Comput. Appl.*, vol. 75, pp. 200–222, 2016.

[2]   A. Rafique, D. Van Landuyt, V. Reniers, and W. Joosen, "Towards an adaptive middleware for efficient multi-cloud data storage," 2017.

[3]   I. Livenson and E. Laure, "Towards Transparent Integration of Heterogeneous Cloud Storage Platforms," 2011.

[4]   S. Kolb and C. Röck, "Unified Cloud Application Management," in *Services (SERVICES), 2016 IEEE World Congress on*, 2016, pp. 1–8.

[5] G. Arunkumar and N. Venkataraman, "A novel approach to address interoperability concern in cloud computing," Procedia Comput. Sci., vol. 50, pp. 554–559, 2015.

[6] E. Alomari, A. Barnawi, and S. Sakr, "Cdport: A framework of data portability in cloud platforms," in Proceedings of the 16th International Conference on Information Integration and Web-based Applications & Services, 2014, pp. 126–133.

[7] "Cloud Storage Initiative | SNIA." [Online]. Available: https://www.snia.org/forums/csi. [Accessed: 05-Jun-2017].

[8]   A. Vijaya and V. Neelanarayanan, "Framework for Platform Agnostic Enterprise Application Development Supporting Multiple Clouds," *Procedia Comput. Sci.*, vol. 50, pp. 73–80, 2015.

[9]   J. Y. Chung, C. Joe-Wong, S. Ha, J. W.-K. Hong, and M. Chiang, "Cyrus: Towards client-defined cloud storage," in *Proceedings of the Tenth European Conference on Computer Systems*, 2015, p. 17.

[10] K. Z. Yin and H. H. Wang, "Mcacm: A cloud storage access control model for multi-clouds environment based on XACML," in *Applied Mechanics and Materials*, 2015, vol. 713, pp. 2451–2454.

[11]   R. Sellami, S. Bhiri, and B. Defude, "Supporting multi data stores applications in cloud environments," *IEEE Trans. Serv. Comput.*, vol. 9, no. 1, pp. 59–71, 2016.

ISBN: 1-60132-458-8, CSREA Press ©

SESSION

DISTRIBUTED COMPUTING AND NOVEL APPLICATIONS + CLUSTER COMPUTING

Chair(s)

TBA

ISBN: 1-60132-458-8, CSREA Press ©

48

Int'l Conf. Grid, Cloud, & Cluster Computing | GCC'17 |

HPC Cluster Management with Open Source Software

Fernando G. Tinetti[1], Leopoldo J. Rios[2]

[1]Fac. de Informática, UNLP, Comisión de Inv. Científicas Prov. Bs. As., La Plata, Argentina
[2]Fac. Ciencias Exactas, UNNE, IMIT-Conicet-UNNE, Corrientes, Argentina

Abstract - *Scientific institutions and laboratories have incorporated and maintain a significant amount of computing resources over the years. Research centers may have unused hardware facilities, with significant processing throughput that could be made available to other institutions. In this paper, we propose a software infrastructure built on existing and new open source software for sharing its computing infrastructure, in a programmed, monitored, and secure way. The Role Based Access Control (RBAC) model is considered a mature and flexible technology, and is a very popular paradigm today. It offers a more secure alternative to the all-or-nothing superuser model. With RBAC, it is possible to apply a specific security policy, and it means that a user has the necessary amount of privileges to perform a task. Taking advantage of the known features of RBAC, it is proposed to add specific HPC monitoring functionality. The HPC monitoring facilities are intended to aid users of scientific programs in their optimization and parallelization tasks of processing intensive jobs.*

Keywords: High Performance Computing, RBAC, Open Source Software, RRDtool, Ganglia.

1 Introduction

In general purpose operating systems such as Linux, it is possible to deploy RBAC technologies to program superuser capabilities in *profiles* or *rights profiles*. These rights profiles are assigned to special user accounts called roles. Then, a user can assume a role to perform a job that requires some of the superuser capabilities. It is possible to configure different predefined rights profiles for different accounts. Rights profiles can provide flexible capabilities for task execution. When creating user roles, it is possible to assign them to some rather wide capabilities range (like that of a superuser), or more restricted capabilities. Specific user permissions are represented as the union of permissions grants that are assigned to user roles [1].

RBAC technology allows to address the possibility of sharing part of the computing infrastructure of an institution. We propose to define a percentage of the equipment to be used by external users, and managed by the software model we present. This software will allow the online monitoring of the occupation of the hardware resources, users, and software

in execution. Fig. 1 schematically shows the idea of sharing an HPC cluster with external users, through the implementation of RBAC policies. The possible configurations are multiple and are adapted to each organization.

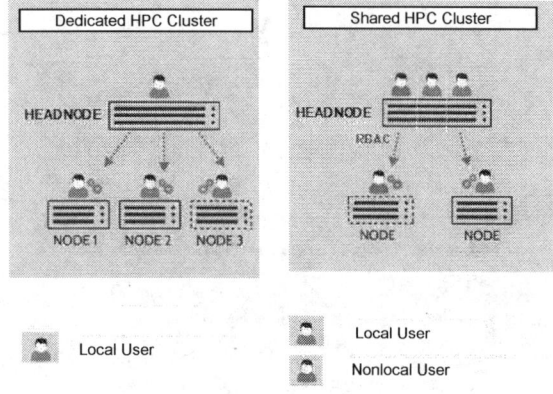

Figure 1: Dedicated and Shared Clusters.

We use a set of definitions/terms in our proposal, which we include here in order to avoid confusions in the rest of the paper:

- HPC cluster: hardware and software infrastructure that allows the concurrent and distributed execution of multiple user program/s in a controlled and monitored environment. A HPC cluster is focused on improving an application performance over and above that provided by a single computer [2].
- Local institution: research/laboratory center having a HPC cluster, which allows nonlocal users to use a fraction of the cluster facilities.
- Local users: local institution researchers and fellows who are granted access to the HPC cluster (computing, storage, etc.) resources.
- Nonlocal users: Researchers and fellows from outside the local institution, who are granted remote controlled access to the HPC cluster (computing, storage, etc.) resources.

We have identified, used, and combined a set of open source software packages [3] with different specific functionalities:

- Operating system (Linux) along with its standard profiling tools (gprof, perf, etc.).

- Batch/job queues processing.
- Job and resources usage monitoring, along with statistics reports.
- Web programming interfaces/web access.
- Database managers.

The first main activity is to program a web interface/access to interact with the nonlocal users of the cluster. Those users should be allowed to edit scripts and execute them, to compile their user programs, and to observe the performance that they obtain. A database will persist every user configuration, as well as the RBAC logistics with user data, access permissions, access times, and permission agreed with each one. The authorities of the local institution will have online information on the actual use of the infrastructure they are sharing, and control of the system for new defining usage policies.

2 Open Source Tools Environment

Our proposal has been implemented using several specific well known software packages, most of them already used (independently of each other) in many HPC clusters:
- 64 bits Linux operating system.
- Torque PBS [4].
- Ganglia [5] combined with RRDtool [6].
- LAMP (MySQL + PHP + Apache) [7].
- CakePHP Framework [8].
- Perf [9].

The Linux distribution is at the user's choice, and corresponds to conform to free distribution and open source standards. For this work, openSUSE has been chosen [10], both for the *headnode* (the cluster front-end node, as shown in Fig. 1), and for the computing nodes. However, it is possible to achieve the same result using any other distributions such as Debian, Ubuntu, or RedHat.

Torque PBS (supported on OpenPBS) is a computing resource manager software that provides control over batch jobs and distributed computing nodes. Torque is considered as open source software using the OpenPBS license, it has Fault Tolerance, Scalability, Scheduling, and Usability features. The essential function of this product is to organize the execution of calculation programs in work allowing a large number of users to run their jobs. An alternative to Torque PBS would be PBS Pro [11], which is a similar open source tool. The basic idea is that jobs run in a cluster - not to in specific nodes - and the queue manager assigns the work to node/s with sufficient resources (mostly RAM and CPU/s). Most queue managers (including OpenPBS) handle parallel and distributed computing programs, where distributed processes communicate through message passing mechanisms [12] [13]. Queue managers, such as OpenPBS naturally handle a cluster with many users, each one with specific job requirements such as RAM amount, sequential

processing, shared memory parallel processing (e.g. with OpenMP threads), and shared memory parallel processing (e.g. with Message Passing Interface -MPI- processes). A configured queuing system ensures all users the execution of their programs, without any taking indefinite use of the nodes, and avoiding runtime resource contention.

Ganglia is a software tool for management of and access statistics of computational resources usage in HPC environments. It is deployed as a web solution, and allows to produce graphs generated on demand, about the actual (cluster wide) use of memory, CPU, and network of an HPC cluster. The proposal that we present includes Ganglia for the general, cluster wide system statistics. However, additional code is integrated to register statistics of use of elements not contemplated in Ganglia, such as the software used, and the distribution of work per user. Ganglia takes advantage of RRDtool for the management of time series data. We have already made some tuning of RRDtool for specific (and different from its default) statistical data sampling [14], later handled and shown in Ganglia web graphics. Cluster wide resource usage statistics/graphics is intended mainly for a role of local institution Director, but it is also possible to grant access to roles such as Researcher and Scholar to observe statistics of their own work.

The RBAC infrastructure programming uses a combination of MySQL [15] (a relational database manager or RDBMS), and CakePHP, a PHP framework widely used in the programming and computing environment. Users have access to the cluster via a web portal where they are handled according to the RBAC policies. Fig. 2 schematically shows the implementation of our RBAC strategy:

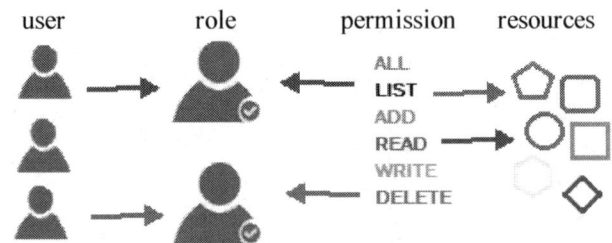

Figure 2: RBAC Strategy.

Authorizations, privileges, and commands with certain security attributes are assigned to profile roles. Roles are, in turn, assigned to users for access control. Our proposal does not make references to linux user accounts, instead, we handle our own (RBAC/web access) user accounts, created in the RBAC database. By default, when a new user is created, this user has no assigned roles, which means that the users does not have access to perform any task behind the RBAC.

Our proposal also includes tools to generate profiling statistics, which are related to but different from Ganglia resource usage reports. Profiling data aids in optimization and parallelization, because it provides data for performance bottlenecks identification, for example. It is possible to produce summary statistics of hardware performance counter, thus aiding in performance evaluation and optimization [16]. Performance analysis based on profiling involves three steps:

- Instrumentation or modification of the program to generate performance data.
- Measurement/sampling of interesting aspects during execution that generate performance data.
- Analysis of runtime collected performance data.

Our proposal integrates scripts available to users, and allows the compilation of source code with specific parameters. The measurement is triggered with the execution of scripts, and the analysis is aiding via personalized monitoring options.

3   Implementation Details and System Functionality

We use a relational database (using MySQL as RDBMS, as explained in the previous section) for maintaining our RBAC system in order to define and enforce users, roles, permissions, etc. Fig. 3 shows our relational database (i.e. tables, keys, etc.), which is relatively simple and does not imply any performance problem.

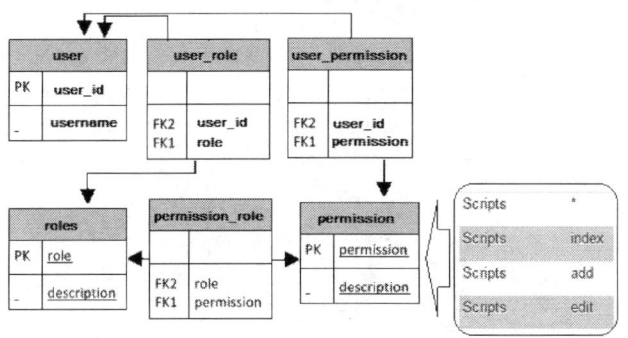

Figure 3: RBAC Database.

Given the relatively small number of users and data involved in permissions and access control (regarding *traditional* databases) the whole system could be implemented on top of files. We have chosen to use MySQL for several reasons:

- Relational databases provide a strong data model/ structure we take advantage of in this specific scenario for RBAC data organization and maintenance.

- Integration with other open source software for web portal implementation/s and web applications deployment.

Every user (disregarding whether a Local or Nonlocal user) interacts with the system through a login process with enabled credentials as shown in Fig. 4. The user 'admin' corresponds to the administrator system/account to manage the entire system, integrates a full menu of options (e.g. for

adding users or changing permissions accesses), as shown in Fig. 5.

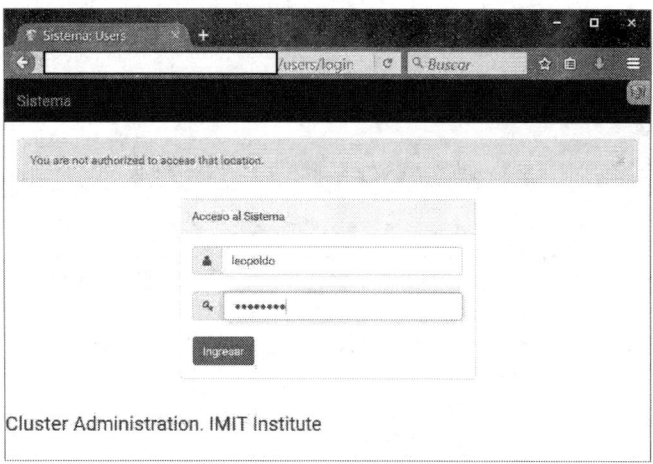

Figure 4: System Login.

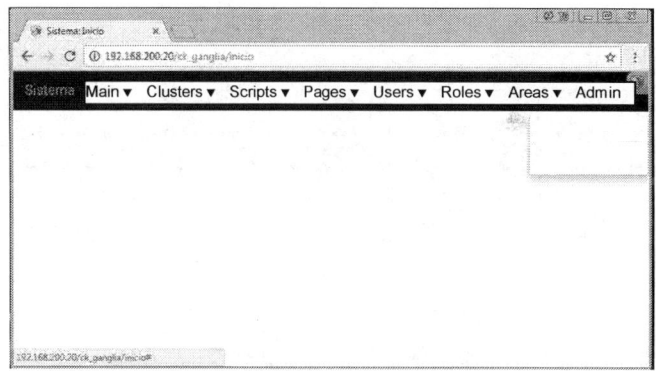

Figure 5: System Administrator Menu.

Roles: Role handling/management is an administrator functionality, and it is used to define and associate roles to system users. The roles defined in our proposal current implementation are: "Becario" (Fellow), "Investigador" (Researcher), "Director" (Director) and "Administrador" (Administrator). Each role assigns permissions to jobs that will be dispatched on resources. User accounts are defined by a name, and its assigned roles (a user account may have more than one role). The user can edit his account profile, as usual, but is not allowed to modify roles (other than the Administrator user). It is possible to program that a user with Fellow role does not have access to visualize cluster usage statistics (a Ganglia resource), if a Director role user so requires. The cluster usage statistics are allowed by default to Researcher and Director roles.

The application allows the system Administrator to assign specific permissions to defined roles. For example, the role "Fellow" is assigned "Scripts / *" permission, which implies access to list, add, and edit scripts of the database. Otherwise, if a role is assigned "Scripts / index" permission, users with this role will only have access to list the available

ISBN: 1-60132-458-8, CSREA Press ©

scripts. Fig. 6 shows that when selecting the "Becario" (Fellow) role it is possible to edit its permissions, initially viewing the current ones. Fig. 7 shows the role edition for this example, i.e. the system reads the current permissions stored in the database and lets the administrator to change them. Once the administrator selects "save", the changes are made permanent by storing them in the database.

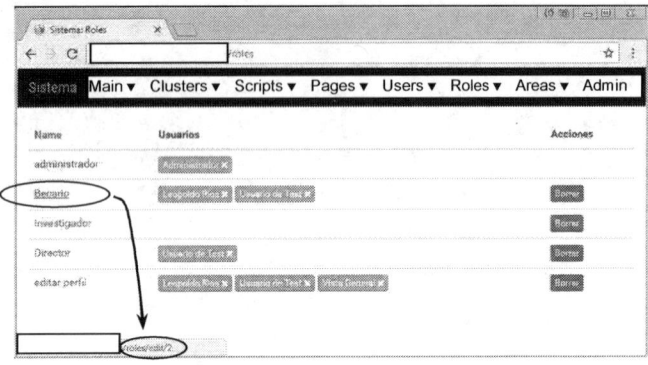

Figure 6: Users and Role Edit.

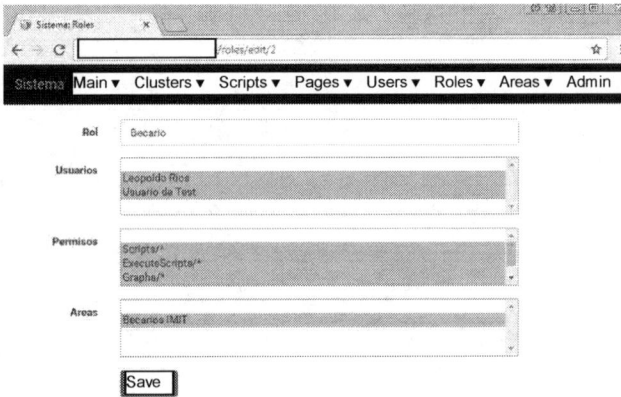

Figure 7: Specific "Becario" Role Edit.

Program execution: the actual usage of the cluster processing facilities is made via the queue manager (Torque PBS, pbs_server application). The user should select some of the available script models and configure the application name, input data, and name of the output file, along with the required CPU and RAM resources. The queue manager, depending on the availability of the resources invoked by the user will determine when to start the execution. During execution, the system reports the status of jobs to users, using monitoring scripts. Once the job is finished, the resulting output files will be stored in temporary folders available to the user. A typical user command line could be:

$ ./user_app input1.dat > stat-out.log

At the end of the execution, the user can visualize their results at the tarminal, or transfer the output file through internet services.

Performance evaluation: Initially, we expect to use the basic profiling tools: gprof, perf, and OProfile [17] [9] [18]. They allow post-mortem analysis. i.e. once the program has ended its runtime it will be possible to analyze several performance indexes (runtime call graph, CPU usage, cache related events, bottlenecks, etc.). The system choses the node on which to run the program along with the specific performance evaluation tool. A user command line, with perf could be:

$ perf stat -e cache-misses ./matmul 1000

which, once completed its runtime in the selected node, will provide the information similar to that shown in Fig. 8. Performance data could be stored in a database, so that the user would be able to analyze not only individual experiments and optimization results but also runtime trends for specific applications and input data sets.

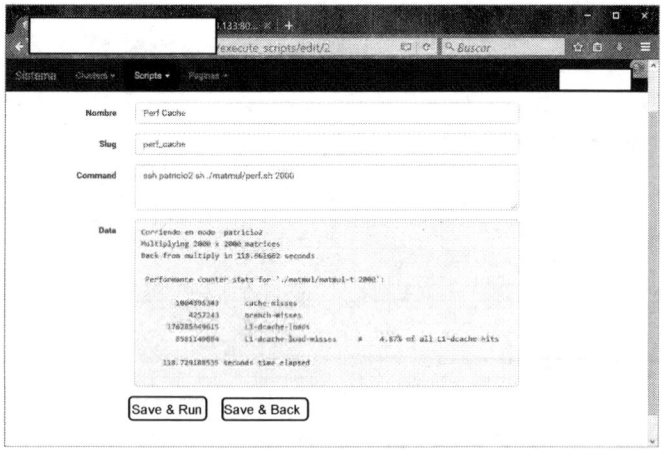

Figure 8: Performance Evaluation Data (perf).

Cluster Sharing and Resource Limits: given that we expect to be able to share a fraction of the HPC cluster resources, we should provide access to nonlocal users. Thus, we should be able to handle security and resource usage details, so that:

- Execution control should be provided to the administrator user/s, for defining application runtime limits, along with computational resources distributed with fairness in amount and usage time.

- External access to the cluster must be assured only to the equipment configured for this purpose. The resto of the hardware should be out of reach of nonlocal users.

- Controlled software installation should be handled by the administrator user/s. The download and compilation of software in the cluster installations must be done or assisted by the cluster administrator, to ensure that their parameterization and configuration does not alter the cluster management and operation.

- User security and control provided basically via the RBAC system, so that each user is isolated and protected, e.g. operations and results are not disclosed and beyond the reach of other users. This requires a detailed programming in the access controls to files and folders, aspect that is considered in the deployment of RBAC.

Specific handling must be implemented for sharing the cluster with nonlocal users. Software techniques such as RBAC for access control and management of external users have been implemented. The control of jobs in the hardware defined as shared is possible either with the job/queue manager already in production (as shown in Fig. 9) or with a new and isolated queue manager (as shown in Fig. 10).

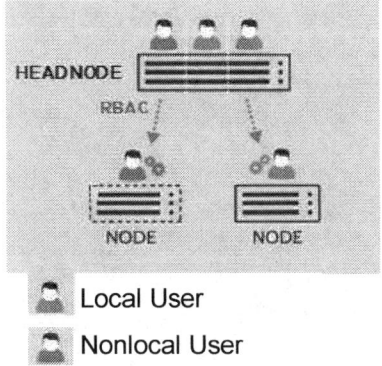

Figure 9: Unified Job Control, Applying RBAC.

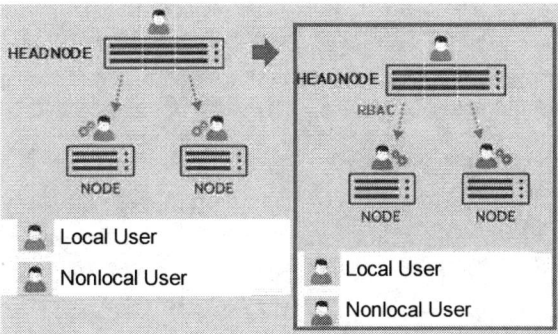

Figure 10: Isolated Job Control, Applying RBAC.

If jobs are handled by a unique job manager, as in Fig. 9, new configurations of users and groups should be defined. Otherwise, if local users' jobs and nonlocal users' jobs are handled with different job managers, then a new standalone manager will be installed in another computer and configure it as the "headnode" of the shared hardware, as shown in Fig. 10.

Security details: The RBAC implementation strategy is supported combining MySQL, Apache, PHP, and CakePHP. Those software technologies along with specific programming determine the correct operation of the proposed system, all of them open source.

The access to resources via web is protected by rules defined for the Apache server. Restrictions and permissions are determined in the ".htaccess" properties for each folder containing resources.

Access to the computer application is controlled by the CakePHP framework. It is not possible to connect to any web portal resource without first doing the login procedure. The model-view-controller chosen for this proposal ensures specific access to predefined views. It can be said that, if something is not programmed in the controller model, it will not be possible to be displayed and used.

In its current version, our proposal does not enable ssh access to users, the users interact with the web system. However, we can change users access in terms of the services allowed from the host "headnode". We can add ssh user acces/ssh user sessions if required. User programs/scripts are stored in the RBAC database, and when the user logs in, they are read and organized in temporary folders for execution.

Runtime constraints: for users in general, and for the "Director" role user/s in particular, it is important to define computational resources usage rules. Runtime limits are useful for preventing single users/user jobs to get resources for an indefinite period of time. Runtime limits are easily defined in job queues of the queue manager tool (Torque PBS in our case). Job queues allow to establish parameters that ensure the correct resource handling in terms of, for example, maximum execution runtime of a job, maximum number of executions per user, users allowed to submit jobs, and maximum number of jobs queued in a cluster, among others. Fig. 11 shows the example configuration of a queue called "cuda".

```
# Create and define queue cuda
#
create queue cuda
set queue cuda queue_type = Execution
set queue cuda max_queuable = 10
set queue cuda max_user_queuable = 10
set queue cuda max_running = 4
set queue cuda resources_default.walltime = 504:00:00
set queue cuda keep_completed = 60
set queue cuda enabled = True
set queue cuda started = True
```

Figure 11: Job Manager Queue Definition: Limits.

Definitions in Fig. 11 are set in the "headnode" of the cluster, and jobs in this queue ("cuda") will be controlled in order to maintain the specific constraints.

4   Conclusions and Further Work

We have been able to combine different open source projects/libraries in order to implement a number of functionalities for HPC cluster management. Our proposal manages local as nonlocal users, so that the HPC cluster/s can be shared among different institutions easily, without the need of complex grid or hybrid clouds software. We are

ISBN: 1-60132-458-8, CSREA Press ©

planning to deploy our development as open source too, once we carefully test our current implementation.

Scalability will be always an issue to analyze, in terms of number of users, fraction of local/nonlocal users, hardware and software resources, etc. Furthermore, we have to carefully experiment on the number of HPC clusters and different sharing options. In the end, we should be able to determine scenarios in which sharing and controlled access will provide specific gains in processing user/scientific jobs.

5   References

[1] Oracle, Oracle Solaris Administration: Security Services, 2012. https://docs.oracle.com/cd/E23824_01/pdf/821-1456.pdf

[2] A. Grama, A. Gupta, G. Karypis, V. Kumar, Introduction to Parallel Computing, 2nd Ed., ISBN: 0-201-64865-2, Addison Wesley, 2003.

[3] Understanding Open Source and Free Software Licensing, Andrew M. St. Laurent, O'Reilly Media, Print: 2004, Ebook: 2008, Ebook ISBN:978-0-596-15308-3.

[4] Adaptive Computing Enterprises, Inc., Torque Resource Manager, Administrator Guide 6.1.0, 2016.

[5] M. Massie, B. Li, B. Nicholes, V. Vuksan, R. Alexander, J. Buchbinder, F. Costa, A. Dean, D. Josephsen, P. Phaal, D. Pocock, Monitoring with Ganglia, O'Reilly Media, SBN: 978-1-4493-2970-9, 2012.

[6] T. Oetiker, About RRDtool, http://oss.oetiker.ch/rrdtool/

[7] J. Lee, B. Ware, Open Source Development with LAMP: Using Linux, Apache, MySQL, Perl, and PHP, Addison-Wesley Professional, ISBN-10: 020177061X, 2002.

[8] R. Dāsa, Learn CakePHP: With Unit Testing, 2nd Ed., Apress, ISBN-10: 1484212134, 2016. https://cakephp.org/

[9] perf: Linux profiling with performance counters, https://perf.wiki.kernel.org.

[10] SUSE LLC, openSUSE - Linux OS. The makers' choice for sysadmins, developers and desktop users, https://www.opensuse.org/

[11] Altair Engineering, Inc., PBS Professional Open Source Project, http://www.pbspro.org/

[12] A. S. Tanenbaum, M. van Steen, Distributed Systems, 3rd Ed., 2017, https://www.distributed-systems.net/index.php/books/distributed-systems-3rd-edition-2017/

[13] Message Passing Interface Forum, MPI: A Message-Passing Interface Standard, Version 3.1, 2015

[14] L. J. Rios, RRDtool data management in HPC Environments (in Spanish), Trabajo de Especialización en Ing. de Software, March 2016, http://sedici.unlp.edu.ar/handle/10915/53669

[15] P. DuBois, MySQL Cookbook: Solutions for Database Developers and Administrators, 3rd Ed., O'Reilly Media, ISBN-10: 1449374026, 2014.

[16] D. J. Lilja, Measuring Computer Performance: A Practitioner's Guide, David J. Lilja, Cambridge University Press, 2000, ISBN 0-521-64670-7.

[17] S. L. Graham, P. B. Kessler, M. K. McKusick, gprof: a call graph execution profiler, ACM SIGPLAN Notices - 20 Years of the ACM SIGPLAN Conference on Programming Language Design and Implementation 1979-1999: A Selection, pp. 49-57, ISSN: 0362-1340, Volume 39 Issue 4, April 2004.

[18] W. E. Cohen, "Tuning Programs with OProfile", Wide Open Magazine, 2004, pages 53-62, https://people.redhat.com/wcohen/Oprofile.pdf

Group Mutual Exclusion Algorithm for Intersection Traffic Control of Autonomous Vehicle

SungHoon Park, BoKyoung Kim, YeongMok Kim
School of Electrical and Computer Engineering, Chungbuk National Unvi. Korea
E-mail: spark@cbnu.ac.kr, agiboss210@naver.com , yeongmokkim@gmail.com

Abstract - *Intersection Traffic Control_(ITC) has attracted extensive attention with the increase of traffic accidents and congestion that has caused huge social and economic losses. The system currently being studied on ITC needs a lot of computations and is based on ans ICU_(Intersection Control Unit) that is neither flexible nor cost efficient. This paper proposes a token-based group mutual algorithm for ITC for autonomous vehicles. To pass the intersection_(IC) safely without an ICU or traffic lights, there should be perfect coordination among autonomous vehicles based on real-time V2V communications. We use two kinds of tokens: a primary token as a privilege and a sub-token as an auxiliary means to increase the performance of vehicle flow. The rational circulation of tokens is the core subject in this algorithm. VTokenIC decreases message complexity and shows better performance in system throughput than existing traffic signal system.*

Keywords : distributed intersection traffic control of autonomous vehicle

1. INTRODUCTION

Intersection Traffic Control_(ITC) has attracted extensive attention with the increase of traffic accidents and congestion that causes a huge social and economic loss. Also the topic on ITC has been widely studied by research communities. These studies fall into two categories: traffic signal scheduling and trajectory maneuver based on an Intersection Central Unit_(ICU). The optimization of signal scheduling needs a lot of computations and the ICU based system is not flexible and cost efficient. To solve this problem a distributed ITC system for autonomous vehicles is a necessary requirement. However, to our knowledge there is almost no work that has been devoted to a distributed ITC for autonomous vehicles. Weigang proposed a distributed mutual exclusion algorithm for intersection control system in 2015. It is valuable that they proposed a distributed ITC system for the first time, but the algorithm needs a lot of messages to be exchanged. We propose a token-based group mutual algorithm for an ITC for autonomous vehicles_(AV) to improve the performance of the distributed ITC system.

2. SYSTEM MODEL AND DEFINITION

The key issue of this proposed algorithm, called VtokenIC, is safe driving and smooth traffic flow through inter-vehicular communication at intersections without a signal system. To pass the intersection_(IC) safely without traffic signals, there should be perfect coordination among vehicles. Vehicles that want to move in the IC should obtain either permission or the privilege to pass the IC.

2.1 system model

We assume a message-passing distributed system comprising a set of n processes AV={AV_1, AV_2,..., AV_n}. All vehicles communicate with each othe by sending messages over a set of channels. The model of the ad-hoc network is defined as an undirected graph.
Each AV has a unique ID and the type of network between AVs is a full network in which one-to-one communication between AVs is possible. We do not consider network trouble and message losses. Also we do not assume any global clock or shared memory.

2.2 The properties of GME

VTokenIC applies GME(Group Mutual Exclusion) theory and the properties of GME for VTokenIC are as below.
(1) safety : If there are more than one AVs' at a Cross Zone_(CZ), those AVs' are catagorized in the same group.
(2) liveness : The vehicle requesting the token eventually enters the CZ.
(3) concurrent entering : In case the requests of all AVs' in an IC belong to the same group, the AV sending a request should not wait till the AVs' in a CZ exit.

2.3 Finite state Automata of AV

In VtokenIC FSA of AV can be presented in a 4-tuple model: AV = (E, S, N, F).
E is physical environment of VTokenIC that contains an IC and lanes. We assume a typical IC with four directions_(North, East, South, West) and 2-lanes each way_(Fig 1). There is a Queuing Zone_(QZ)) and CZ in the IC.

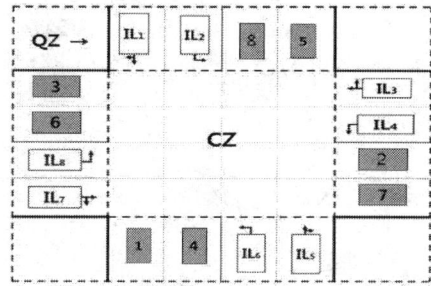

Fig 1. intersection

ISBN: 1-60132-458-8, CSREA Press ©

An AV, if it wants to pass a CZ, should enter the QZ and wait until it gains the privilege to enter the CZ. The QZ consists of 8 ILs and each IL is numbered from 1 to 8. The direction of the AV is decided by the IL it is at and the AVs in the odd numbered ILs can move forward and turn right and in even numbered IL they can only turn left.

The QZ and the CZ consist of grids and AVs should move forward to the grids of the QZ and CZ according to the grid rule that applies to all AVs in the IC consecutively. AVs can move forward one grid if the state of the front grid_(the neighborhood) is off_(empty).

Definition 1. The compatible and conflict relationship
If AVs pass the CZ simultaneously, there would be a crash therefore AVs crossing the CZ lanes should pass the CZ mutual exclusively. These AVs are in a conflict relationship. AVs with non-crossing lanes can pass the CZ simultaneously. These AVs and their lanes are in compatible relationship.

Definition 2 Compatible Lane Group_(CLG)
When ILs are compatible with each other, we call the set of these ILs CLG. An example of CLG is given in table 1.

table 1. CLG

CLG	IL	CLG		
CLG1	IL_1-str	IL_5-str	IL_5-right	IL_1-right
CLG2	IL_2-left	IL_6-left		
CLG3	IL_3-str	IL_7-str	IL_7-right	IL_3-right
CLG4	IL_4-left	IL_8-left		
CLG5	IL_5-str	IL_1-str	IL_1-right	IL_5-right
CLG6	IL_6-left	IL_2-left		
CLG7	IL_7-str	IL_3-str	IL_7-right	IL_3-right
CLG8	IL_8-left	IL_4-left		

*str : straight

S is the state of AVs that can be changed according to the movement and location of the AV. The state of an AV is classified as approaching, waiting (w-move and w-CZ) or passing as shown in Fig 2.

Fig 2. state of AV
N is the input of the information from a sensor and the GPS installed in the AV and the messages between the AVs.
F is the functions related to the movement and the control of the AV in the IC.

3. PROTOCOL OF VTOKENIC

3.1 Framework of VTokenIC

VtokenIC is a distributed mutual exclusion algorithm designed to control AVs in an IC without a signal system.

(1) VtokenIC is a token-based ME algorithm
VtokenIC uses a token as an indication of the privilege to pass an IC; how to circulate the token is the core of VtokenIC. We use two kinds of tokens: a primary token and a sub-token. A primary token is given to the leader of a session and the primary token holder can enter the critical section as the leader. A prime token holder generates a sub-token and give it to the captain of the concurrent lane. The sub-token is an auxiliary means to increase the performance

of the system flow. Therefore, the efficient circulation of the main token and the systematic management of the sub-token are the core of VtokenIC.

(2) VtokenIC is an algorithm designed for the movement of AVs and the flow of sessions. VTokenIC is based on the circulation of the main token and the consecutive flow of sessions. A session is a time-interval in which the main token holder and the vehicles in the same group with the main token holder pass a CZ together.

·$session_i$ = {pti-holder, pti.holder-ch.mem, sti-holder, sti.holder-ch.mem}
·$session_i$ start:
{(pti-1)-holder, (pti-1).holder-ch.mem} $\cup$
{(sti-1)-holder, (sti-1).holder-ch.mem} = {}
·$session_i$ termination $\rightarrow$ $session_{i+1}$ start
{pti-holder, pti.holder-ch.mem} $\cup$
{sti-holder, sti.holder-ch.mem} = {}

$Session_i$ starts when all AVs of the previous session, $session_{i-1}$, leave the CZ. And $session_i$ is terminated when all AVs in the CZ leave the CZ and the next session, $session_{i+1}$, is started when the main token is sent to the next token holder. When the primary token holder is changed, all AVs in the same group can join its session. VTokenIC is the algorithm for the consecutive flow of sessions as shown in Fig 3.

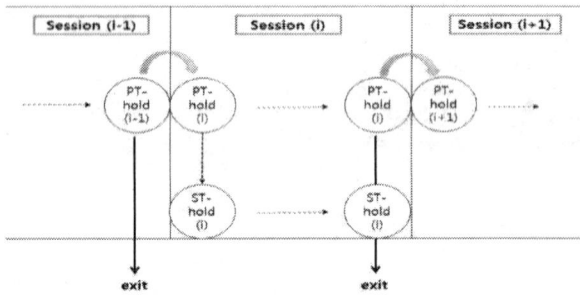

Fig 3. the flow of sessions

3.2 Description of VTokenIC

Each vehicle in a session goes through 3 sections to pass IC as shown Fig 4. Fig 4. VTokenIC

(1) Entry section
When AVi, approaching an IC, enters the QZ it receives a signal from the QZ border. AVi then broadcasts request the message to all AVs in the IC.
If AVi is the captain of ELi, it sends an ack message to AVj when it receives the request. Otherwise it neglects the ack message received.
When AVs receive ack messages from the captain of

Int'l Conf. Grid, Cloud, & Cluster Computing | GCC'17 |

57

ELi, AVi becomes a member of the ELi chain. AVi moves forward to ELi according to the grid rules and the state of AVi is changed to w-CZ from w-move.

However if AVi does not receive an ack message, it becomes the captain of ELi when it arrives at the boundary of CZ. The state of AVi is changed to w-CZ from w-move and AVi sends ack messages to all AVs in ILi (Fig 5).

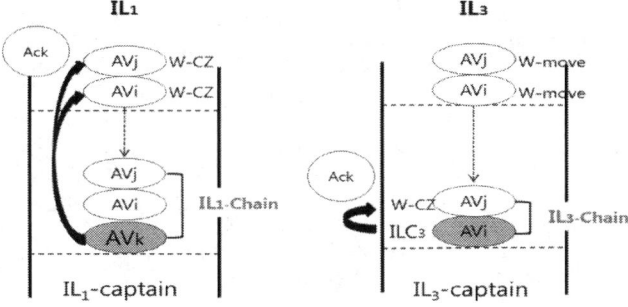

Fig 5. IL chain

(2) Core Section

This section shows how AVi enters a CZ. When the captain of an EL receives the main token, it becomes a token-holder and gets the privilege to enter the CZ. Since then the AVi starts the CZ entering procedure. AVi selects CSGi in Fig 5 which passes CZ with AVi and generates a sub-token and sends it to the captain of the selected IL. However the token-holder can not enter the CZ immediately in case there are some vehicles of the previous session remaining in the CZ. The token-holder should check that all the vehicles of previous session leave the CZ. The safety check can be done by a GPS device installed in the AVi. When the CZ is empty, the prime token-holder enters the CZ and the state of the AV is changed to "passing".

If AVi receives a sub-token from the primary token holder, AVi becomes a sub-token holder and enter the CZ just after the primary token holder enter the CZ.

When the prime token holder and sub-token holder enters the CZ, they move in a group with their chain members together.

(3) Exit Section

When AVi meets the exit boundary of a CZ, it has to exit and cannot wait in the CZ. AVi should transfer the main token to the next ,selected holder(Fig 6). Here, how to transfer the main token is critical to the performance of the algorithm. VTokenIC applies the roundabout method presented in table 2.

table 2. sequence of PT

seq	IL	seq	IL
①	IL1-str	⑤	IL5-str
②	IL2-left	⑥	IL6-left
③	IL3-str	⑦	IL7-str
④	IL4-left	⑧	IL8-left

*seq : sequence

If the prime token holder is in EL1, it transfers the prime token to the captain of EL2_(the next-holder) when it

exits the boundary. But in case there is no vehicle in EL2, it sends the token to the last vehicle of EL1 chain temporarily and exits.

Also when the temporal token holder arrives at the boundary, it transfers the token to the captain of EL2. But in case there are no vehicles in EL2, it sends the token to the last vehicle of EL5(the concurrent lane) chain temporarily and exit.

Again when the temporal token holder arrives at the boundary, it transfers the token to the captain of EL2 and exits. But in case there are no vehicle in EL2, the temporal token holder should check all the rest of the 7 ELs'. In case there is no AV at the other 7 ELs', it discards the token and exits the CZ. In another case, it sends the token to the first

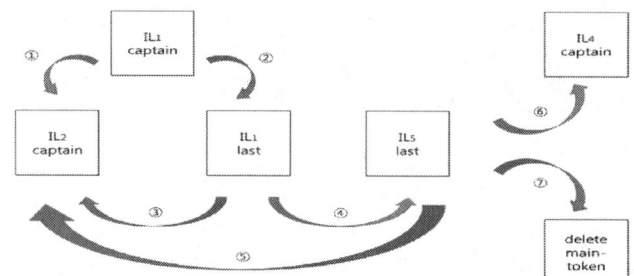

EL among the 7 ELs', which has a pending request.

Fig 6. circulation of PT

4. PERFORMANCE ANALYSI

The performance measures are message complexity, synchronization delay and concurrency.

4.1 message complexity

VTokenIC exchanges 8 kinds of messages and the message complexity of VTokenIC in the worst case is $1.125n+5$. The scenario of the worst case is given as follows:
(1) AVi broadcasts a request message to each AV in the IC : $(n-1)$
(2) The captain of ELi sends a ack message in response to the request : $0.125n(1n/8)$
(3) when AVi, the prime token holder, enters CZ : 3
(4) when AVi exits CZ : 3

On the otherhand in case AVi is a chain member of ILi, only n messages are needed.

4.2 Synchronization delay

Synchronization delay is defined as the time between two consecutive sessions. The Synchronization delay of VTokenICs is $2t$ when t is the maximum message delay.

4.3 Concurrency

Concurrency will be n in case all the AVs' want to join the same session simultaneously.
There are 8 ELs' in IC and if there are the same number of vehicles in each EL, the concurrency of VTokenIC is $n/4$.
The performance of VTokenIC can be presented as table 3..

table 3. performance of VTokenIC

	mc	sd	cr
VTokenIC	$1.125n+5$	t	$n/8$

ISBN: 1-60132-458-8, CSREA Press ©

Mamun	$n+2$	$2t$	n
Mittal	$2n-1$	t	n
Weigang	$3n$		$n/8$
Kakugawa	$5Q+1$	$3-4t$	n

*mc: message complexity / sd: synchronization delay / cr: concurrency

5. CONCLUSION

VTokenIC decreases message complexity by using an IL-chain concept. The results of simulation show that VTokenIC can handle a large traffic volume well with decreased message complexity. This is due to the rational circulation of tokens. This paper can vitalize research into distributed ITCs, but. further studies into VTokenIC are necessary to improve it.

6. References

[1] Weigang Wu, Jiebin Zhang, Aoxue Luo, Jiannong Cao, A distributed mutual exclusion algorithm for intersection traffic control, IEEE transactions on parallel ans distributed systems, vol 26, Jan. 2015

[2] Quazi Ehsanul Kabir Mamun, Hidenori Nagazato, A new token based protocol for group mutual exclusion in distributed systems, Proceedings of the fifth international symposium(ICPDC 2006)

[3] Neeraj Mittal, Prajwal K. Mohan, A priority-based distributed group mutual exclusion algorithm when grpup access is non-uniform, J. Parallel Distrib. comput, 2007

[4] Hirotsugu Kakugama, Sayaka kemei, Toshimitsu Masuzawa, A tpken based distributed group mutual exclusion with quorums, IEEE transactions on parallel ans distributed systems, vol 19, Sep. 2008

[5] Fei Yan, Mahjoub DRIDI, Abdellah el Moudni (2013). "An autonomous vehicle sequencing problem at intersections: A genetic algorithm approach" Int.J.Appl. Math. Comput. Sci,. 2013, No1, 183-200.

[6] Md. Abdus Samad Kamal, Jun-ichi Imura, Tomohisa Hayakawa, Akira Ohata (2015) "A vehicle-Intersection Coordination Scheme for Smooth flows of traffic without using traffic lights". IEEE Transactions on parallel and distributed systems, vol. 16. No3, June 2015

[7] Li Li, Fei-Yue Wang (2006) "Cooperative driving blind crossing using intervehicle communication". IEEE Transactions on parallel and distributed systems, vol. 55. No6, November 2006 추가

[8] Mamotu Maekawa (1985), "A root N algorithm for mutual exclusion in decentralized systems" ACM Transaction on programming languages and systems, vol 3, No 2, May 1985, page 145-159

[9] Kerry Raymond (1989), "A tree-based algorithm for distributed mutual exclusion" ACM Transaction on programming languages and systems, vol 7, No 1, Feb 1989, page 61-77

ISBN: 1-60132-458-8, CSREA Press ©

Cost-Efficiency Comparison of an ARM Cluster & Intel Server

Jaden D. Weiss
High Technology High School
Lincroft, NJ, USA

Abstract - *Data processing requirements can be met by using a small group of complex fast processors or a large number of extremely low-cost and low-power processors. This paper empirically compares the cost-effectiveness of these two computing paradigms and evaluates the hypothesis that the low-cost processor solution is more cost-effective. The control group consists of data obtained from a traditional Intel server (2 Intel Xeon CPUs) and the experimental group consists of data obtained from an ARM cluster—6 low-cost Orange Pi One single-board-computers using ARM processors. The ARM cluster was found to be significantly more cost-efficient than the traditional Intel server.*

Keywords: cluster computing, ARM, cost

1 Introduction

Computing needs can be met by using a variety of hardware solutions. Cost is typically a key factor and this is especially true for massive data processing tasks such as indexing the World Wide Web. In this paper we compare the cost efficiency of two very different computing solutions: a cluster of low cost ARM processors versus a much smaller number of fast, but more costly, Intel servers. Industry typically favors the Intel solution, but we hypothesize that the ARM solution is more cost efficient. Prior work has shown mixed results. One study indicated that ARM processors are not as efficient at High Performance Computing tasks [2]. However, another study demonstrated that some general purpose computing tasks are more efficient when using the ARM processors [3].

Companies such as Google need to constantly process webpages in order to maintain an up-to-date database to support web searches [4]. Processing this constant influx of new or modified web pages requires a large amount of processing power, and hence web page indexing is a relevant and important data processing task. In this paper we use a web indexing task as our processing benchmark for comparing the relative cost effectiveness of the ARM and Intel solutions.

For this study we constructed an ARM cluster using 6 Orange Pi One Single-Board Computers (SBCs) and compared its performance against that of an Intel Server. The benchmark web page indexing task was executed on both computing solutions and the cost efficiency for each solution

was determined. Our results indicate that the ARM cluster is significantly more cost-effective than the Intel server solution.

This paper is organized as follows. Section 2 describes the two processor architectures that are evaluated as well as the cluster design. Section 3 provides a detailed description of the benchmark web indexing task and Section 4 provides our main results. Our conclusion are provided in Section 5.

2 Processor Architectures

In this Section we compare the current Intel and ARM Cortex-A7 microarchitectures, as well as describe the Single-Board Computer chosen for the comparison. The Orange Pi One (see Figure 1) was chosen as our low cost solution because each unit only costs $9.99, has reasonable performance due to its four ARM Cortex-A7 cores, and its 100M Ethernet provides decent networking capabilities.

Figure 1: Orange Pi One SbBC with ARM processor

Originally designed as a low power multicore architecture for Android smartphones/tablets, the ARM Cortex-A7 uses a minimalist pipeline in order to efficiently handle a large number of low activity background tasks. This is in contrast to the Intel processors, which are designed to handle a smaller number of high intensity foreground tasks, with a deep pipeline and individual L2 caches for each core. However, the deeply pipelined design of the Intel processor may decrease performance when handling a large number of tasks. Webpage indexing involves a large number of simultaneously executing tasks—with hundreds or even thousands of threads—and hence the ARM processor might be better designed for such tasks. Table 1 provides some detailed information about both processors.

Table 1: Comparison of Intel vs. ARM Architectures

	INTEL	ARM CORTEX-A7
μOP/clock	8	2
SIMD	128-bit x2	64-bit shared
Pipeline Depth	20-24 stages	8 stages
L2 Cache	Individual	Shared 4 cores
Data Width	64-bit	32-bit

The ARM cluster uses 6 Orange Pi One Single Board Computers (SBCs). Each of these Orange Pi Ones has 4 ARM Cortex-A7 cores, assorted coprocessors, a Cat-5 networking port, 512 MB of RAM, and a GPU (unused). The Orange Pi Ones do not have fans; instead they are passively cooled. An 8 port networking hub is used to connect these SBCs together and to provide access to the Internet. The constructed ARM cluster has a total cost of $200. The Intel Server uses 2 Quad-Core Intel Xeon processors and is actively cooled. The Intel server used in this study has a total cost of $2,535. One important difference between the ARM and Intel solution is that for ARM solution the peripherals (most importantly the network controller) are integrated directly into the SoC of the Orange Pi One, whereas for the Intel server they are connected over PCIe. This gives the Orange Pi One and the ARM solution higher performance when accessing peripherals (i.e. networking), which is important for our web pages benchmarking task that requires intensive network access.

Feature-wise, the ARM and Intel solutions are very similar. Both support hardware-accelerated virtualization. All ARM Cortex-A processors have supported this feature—even those designed for smartwatches and set-top boxes. The SoC used in the Orange Pi One and the Intel CPU both support acceleration for the AES encryption algorithm. The SoC in the Orange Pi One also supports several other common cryptographic algorithms.

3   Benchmark

In order to compare the cost effectiveness of the two computing solutions, a benchmark program was written to index Wikipedia pages. Wikipedia was chosen for its relatively uniform page structure and reliable ping times, as well as its wealth of available URLs for extraction. The indexing program was written in Google Go [1] because it has an efficient HTML tokenizer and an efficient concurrency system that allows it to handle the large number of pages that must be indexed concurrently.

This indexing process, which is shown in Figure 2, occurs in the following sequence. First, the link is sent to the indexer (second rectangle from the bottom in the second column in Figure 2). Then the indexer extracts the title of the web page, a list of words as well as their frequency of occurrence, a list of headings, a list of the text paragraphs, and a list of hyperlinks along with the associated text describing them. The resulting page data is then sent to the page recurser which iterates through the links and sends the Wikipedia links to the hash distributer. The hash distributer then hashes the links and the hash value is used to route the links to the appropriate node (either the Intel server or one of the Orange Pi Ones). Next, the deduplicators store a list of links in order to prevent them from being repeatedly reindexed. The links that were not previously indexed are placed into a buffer. The output of this buffer is automatically distributed among all of the nodes. These links are then sent to the indexers and the process continues. All channels (the labelled arrows in Figure 2) are buffered in order to prevent any part of the indexing pipeline from needing to wait for more work to do.

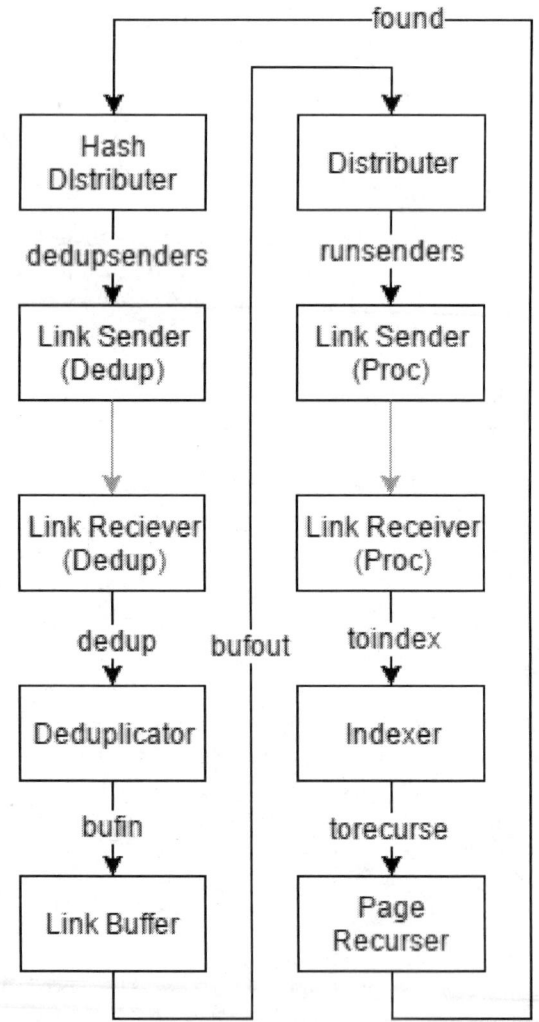

Figure 2: Flowchart of Web Page Indexing Benchmark

ISBN: 1-60132-458-8, CSREA Press ©

The indexer was started and then allowed to run for 2 minutes. After the 2 minutes, the number of links processed was recorded for each node and sent to the control node, which saved it to a file. All data sent over the network was encoded with gob (a high performance binary protocol for Google Go).

The benchmark program is executed 12 times on both the Intel server and the ARM cluster. On the Intel server, 200 pages were indexed concurrently per core, while on the ARM cluster 10 pages were indexed concurrently per core. These values were selected because we determined that they were the highest values that did not lead to connection timeouts.

4 Results

The benchmark was run 12 times on the ARM cluster and Intel server in order to obtain a sample size sufficient for statistical analysis. After the benchmark runs were completed, the results were recorded and analyzed. The results for the 12 runs are displayed in Table 2. The "Pages" field specifies the total number of pages indexed in the 2 minute period. The speed in pages per second (Pages/s) was then calculated by dividing the total number of pages indexed in this two minute period by 120. Finally, the cost effectiveness ($/Page/s) was calculated by dividing the cost of the computing solution by the speed in Pages/s. Recall that the cost of the ARM cluster is $200 and the cost of the Intel server is $2,535.

Table 2: Web Indexing Benchmark Results

	ARM			INTEL		
Run	Pages	Pages/s	$/Page/s	Pages	Pages/s	$/Page/s
1	7,739	64.49	3.10	21,286	177.38	14.30
2	6,636	55.30	3.62	20,193	168.28	15.07
3	8,104	67.53	2.96	19,550	162.92	15.57
4	6,458	53.82	3.72	21,442	178.68	14.19
5	8,223	68.53	2.92	19,658	163.82	15.48
6	8,441	70.34	2.85	16,773	139.78	18.14
7	8,538	71.15	2.81	21,331	177.76	14.27
8	7,710	64.25	3.12	17,202	143.35	17.69
9	8,774	73.12	2.74	17,636	146.97	17.26
10	7,116	59.30	3.38	17,426	145.22	17.46
11	8,273	68.94	2.90	19,768	164.73	15.39
12	8,614	71.78	2.79	20,607	171.73	14.77
Avg.	7,886	65.71	3.08	19,406	161.72	15.80

The results in Table 2 show that, despite being approximately 13 times ($2535/$200) as expensive as the ARM cluster, the Intel server is on average only ~2.5x faster (161.72/65.71). Therefore, the ARM cluster is 5.13 (15.80/3.08) times as cost effective as the Intel server. In order to match the Intel server's cost effectiveness, the ARM cluster would need to be upgraded to accommodate 15 Orange Pi One SBCs—which would cost only $362.13.

Table 3: Summary Data Table for Cost per Unit Work ($/Page/s)

	ARM	INTEL
n	12	12
Mean	3.08	15.80
Standard Dev	0.31	1.39

Table 3 shows the summary cost-effectiveness statistics over the 12 runs. Clearly the mean cost per unit work for the ARM solution is much lower than for the Intel solution. A two-tailed t-test indicates that the results are statistically significant with $p=8.3\times10^{-13}$.

5 Conclusion

This research shows that for general performance computing tasks (which involve processing of network data rather than intense mathematical processing) the ARM Cortex-A7 is more cost effective than Intel processors. Industry may be finally ready to exploit this advantage. Very recently (while this study was being conducted), a cloud computing company called Scaleway added ARM severs to their datacenters in order to deliver cheaper VMs and bare-metal servers than their competitors. Scaleway sells ARM servers with 4 CPU cores, 2GB of memory, and 50GB of SSD for €2.99/month ($3.27/month at the time of writing), either as bare-metal or a virtual machine. However, Scaleway only has datacenters in Paris and Amsterdam, and very few other large cloud hosting companies have adopted ARM servers.

There are also many other characteristics of ARM processors which may work well at large scale—including low power consumption, low heat output, and low hardware maintenance requirements. ARM has also released a new core (ARM Cortex-A35) which is faster and more efficient than the Cortex-A7. This will likely make the ARM even more cost effective than the Intel solution, but no devices are available using this core at the time of writing this. There are also many other ARM SBCs and cores which can be compared.

6 References

[1] I. Balbaert. The Way to Go: A Thorough Introduction to the Go Programming Language. IUniverse, 2012.

[2] M. F. Cloutier, C. Paradis, and V. M. Weaver. Design and Analysis of a 32-bit Embedded High-Performance Cluster Optimized for Energy and Performance. In *Proceedings of the 1st International Workshop on Hardware-Software Co-Design for High Performance Computing,* pp. 1-8, New Orleans, LA, IEEE, 2014.

[3] Z. Ou, B. Pang, Y. Deng, J. K. Nurminen, A. Yla-Jaaski, and P. Hui. Energy- and Cost-Efficiency Analysis of ARM-Based Clusters. In *Proceedings of the 12th IEEE/ACM International Symposium on Cluster, Cloud and Grid Computing,* pp. 115-123, Washington, DC: IEEE Computer Society, 2012.

[4] L. Page, S. Brin, R. Motwani, and T. Winograd. The PageRank Citation Ranking: Bringing Order to the Web, Stanford InfoLab, 1999.

SESSION

POSTER PAPERS

Chair(s)

TBA

Design of a tool for analyzing supercomputer status using a integrated log repository

Sung-Jun Kim[1]**, Jae-Kook Lee**[1]**, and Tae-Young Hong**[1]

[1]Supercomputing Center, Korea Institute of Science and technology Information, DaeJeon, Rep. of KOERA

Abstract - Large scale clusters like supercomputers are composed of various elements, including computational nodes, filesystems, and interconnected networks. Researchers dispatch their parallelized jobs to computational nodes. Determining whether such computations are being efficiently conducted by the supercomputer, which is composed of thousands of nodes, is a difficult task for system managers. In this study, a integrated log repository was designed to improve efficiency of supercomputer use by integrating the storage of various different logs generated by the supercomputer. The usefulness of the proposed system will be explain by investigating scenarios of supercomputer status analysis systems to be developed in the near future.

Keywords: supercomputer, log, analysis

1   Introduction

The Supercomputing Center of the Korea Institute of Science and Technology Information (KISTI) provides large scale supercomputers for domestic researchers. Researchers prepare parallel programming for their scientific computations which are then delivered to the batch job scheduler program (hereafter, the scheduler) of the supercomputer. Then, the scheduler allocates the task to idle computational resources.

There are cases where the computational resource is not efficiently taken advantage of, depending on the characteristics or quality of the program prepared by the researcher. In such cases, the necessary computation times are greater, which can result in the researcher not being able to produce the sought-after research results within the time given. As a result of the inefficient management of resources from the perspective of the service center, opportunities to provide the service to more researchers are reduced.

Currently, the service center monitors system utilization using cluster monitoring programs like Ganglia and other in-house developed tools, while regularly managing the operational efficiency by examining statistical data.

However, existing monitoring tools are not able to link the researcher tasks with the system utilization data, so system managers need to determine the system status by separately looking at the information produced by each corresponding tool.

In this paper, a integrated log repository was designed to allow the efficiency of the entire system to be conveniently determined with respect to the researcher tasks, by integrating the user task information collected through the scheduler with the system utilization data obtained from monitoring tools such as Ganglia. The composition of the repository proposed in this study is expected to be used when a supercomputer status analysis tool is implemented in the future.

2   Related Works

2.1   SGE(Sun Grid Engine)

<Table 1> shows the accounting information from the log generated by SGE. It contains userid, node information used by the jobs, and the resource usages of the jobs.

<Table 1> Accounting information of SGE

queue	wait time	cpu time
exec_host	run time	job option
group	mem usage	exit code
userid	vmem usage	pe_taskid
job id	number of cpu	job name
submit time	start time	end time

2.2   Ganglia

Ganglia is a representative cluster monitoring tool. This tool is composed of gmond, which monitors the performance data of each node, and gmetad, which collects and stores that performance data. <Table 2> shows some of the node performance information monitored through gmond.

<Table 2> Ganglia Monitoring Metrics

	Monitoring metrics
CPU	Idle, User, System, wio
DISK	Space available, Total disk space
Load	Load {one | five | fifteen }
Memory	Buffers, Cached, Free, Shared
Network	{Byte|Packet} {Received|Sent}

ISBN: 1-60132-458-8, CSREA Press ©

3   System Design

As discussed earlier, SGE includes information related to the researcher jobs, and Ganglia include information regarding the status of nodes. However, the efficient operation of the system requires a comprehensive determination of the data from SGE and Ganglia, followed by an appropriate response. To do this, a log integrated repository for the supercomputer status analysis was designed, as shown in <Figure 1>.   By analyzing and storing the relationships between the logs, this method will allow both usage status determination and statistics computation.

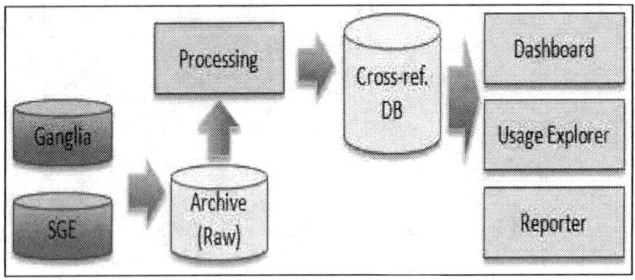

<Figure 1> System Architecture

The above system can be used to identify information that is difficult to assess using the existing development monitoring tools.

<Table 3> Scenario 1

Scenario 1	Actual CPU utilization status for the computational node used by a specific researcher's task
Reference Information	SGE : researcher ID, task allocated node information, task start time, task end time Ganglia: measurement time, CPU load information
Predicted display	

The above <Table 3> shows an example of a display composition that is possible using the log integrated repository designed in this study. It is expected that this approach will allow the display of data that is presently difficult to determine using existing, individual monitoring tools.

It is important to be able to identify problems involving a specific researcher task when it is not properly utilizing the computational nodes. By determining such problems and modifying the researcher task programming, the system's task efficiency and utilization rate can be improved.   In addition, by displaying the relationship between the loads of the filesystem or network in graph form, the effect of the relationship between the researcher task and the system can be more conveniently determined.

The database for the log storage will use a NoSQL database like MongoDB, which is more appropriate for irregular data storage compared with a conventional relational database. This will minimize the number of logs generated and the waste of data produced when performing standardization. Also, this was done to define the data schema to allow a more convenient display of the data.

Moreover, by collecting the calculated daily results in advance into batch operation form and storing the data, the time needed for report generation can be reduced, while also reducing the query time for report generation.

4   Conclusions

In this paper, we design an analysis tool that integrates and stores the logs of both the batch job scheduler program (SGE) and performance monitoring tool (Ganglia) related to the utilization of the supercomputer. The objective of combining the logs is to produce information that is otherwise difficult to identify using existing individual monitoring tools.

In the future, it is expected that a real system based on the proposed design will be established, and will allow convenient monitoring and analysis of the system utilization status by the system manager. Furthermore, application of this system is predicted to significantly improve the researcher task efficiency and system utilization.

5   References

[1]   Ganglia Monitoring System, http://ganglia.info

[2]   Sun Grid Engine Account file Format, http://gridscheduler.sourceforge.net/htmlman/htmlman5/accounting.html

[3]   S.J Kim, et al, "Analysis of user batch job statistics to maximize HPC resource usage", ICSMB,pp323-324, 2016

[4]   S.J Kim, et al, "User job pattern analysis of KISTI 4th SMP Supercomputer", ICCT2016, pp.1076-1077, 2016

ISBN: 1-60132-458-8, CSREA Press ©

Correlation Analysis of OpenStack Log using Machine Learning Techniques

Ju-Won Park[1] **and Eunhye Kim**[2]

[1]Div. of Supercomputing, KISTI, Daejeon, Republic of Korea

[2]Hyper-connected Communication Research Lab, ETRI, Daejeon, Republic of Korea

Abstract— *To maintain the health of system, administrator usually analyzes event logs to figure out the problem and sort it out since the event logs contains the relevant message that enables the administrator to infer the cause of the error. However, it is almost impossible for administrators to analyze event log files one by one to identify the cause of an error since recent systems are huge and complex. In this paper, we present correlation analysis approach between OpenStack logs using machine learning method. Specifically, this paper 1) collects event log, 2) conducts the normalization of collected log messages, 3) clusters the collected data using unsupervised machine learning method, and 4) analyzes correlations among the clustered message group based on Dynamic Time Warping (DTW).*

Keywords: Machine learning, correlation, openstack log, message-based analysis.

1. Introduction

In the event of an error in a system, administrator usually analyzes event log to identify the cause of the error since the event log contains severity level information (e.g., Warning, Error, and Critical) along with the relevant phrases that enables the administrator to infer the cause of the error. However, today's systems accordingly generate a considerable amount of log message and complex relationships among system modules, so it is almost impossible for administrators to analyze event logs one by one to identify the cause of an error. In particular, as OpenStack [1], which is being widely used for providing open-source based cloud service, is composed of various service modules such as NOVA, NEUTRON, and KEYSTONE being linked to distributed multiple servers, it is hard to access each node and analyze event logs for each service module in the case of an error.

In this regard, this paper presents message-based log analysis method that enables the administrator to find the cause of an error quickly. Study process is as follows: First, event logs occurred in both a system level and application service level from multiple servers are collected and then transferred to a single collection server to collect dispersed event log data. Second, normalization is conducted to grasp the semantic context of log messages and improve the accuracy of analysis. Third, the normalized messages are clustered through the hierarchical clustering method. Last,

the correlation among clustered message groups is analyzed by using the Dynamic Time Warping (DTW) method [2].

2. Proposed approach

In OpenStack, which is a cloud management platform, event logs are stored in different files depending on executed service. For instance, NOVA service installed in computing node save logs in the */var/log/nova* file, while NEUTRON displays logs in the */var/log/neutron* file. Therefore, to collect the logs in single server from distributed multiple systems, this paper utilizes rsyslog [3]. Specifically, OpenStack event logs are saved in system log file (*/var/log/message*). Then, system logs are transmitted to server using rsyslog client daemon.

To extract an important phrase, normalization process is required, as suggested by [4], [5]. First is to convert all characters to small letters. Second is to delete symbols, numbers, and prepositions, which do not have meaning. For example, accuracy of clustering can increase by eliminating symbols (e.g., -, +, ?, [, and !) and weak words (e.g., a, the, of, such and from). Third is to eliminate unique values such as ID. In OpenStack, each virtual instance has its ID for management. Therefore, as event logs for the same event have different instance ID, ID needs to be removed. Forth is to replace directory path with PATH. OpenStack logs include a number of directory paths, but in most cases, it indicates not the cause of error but the location of files. Therefore, clustering by replacing directory path with PATH can increase accuracy.

To sort out the normalized messages by similarity of meaning, all messages are separated by word, and converted into metric representing use of words and frequency. Since the converted metric is represented in numeric showing frequency of used words, Euclidean distance can be measured. Based on the distance, similarity was analyzed by using the hierarchical clustering analysis method which is employed to find the clustering boundaries from the weight vectors. Each step of message-based clustering is detailed in the following. Let $M = (m_1, m_2, \ldots, m_n)$ be a set of messages and $T = (t_1, t_2, \ldots, t_n)$ be a set of distinct terms in M.

1) Compute the similarity between all pairs of clusters

using (1).

$$S(t_\alpha, t_\beta) = \left(\sum_p^{t=1} |f_{\alpha,t} - f_{\beta,t}|^2 \right)^{1/2} \quad (1)$$

where two messages m_α and m_β is represented by their term vectors t_α and t_β respectively. $f_{m,t}$ denotes the frequency of term $t \in T$ in message $m \in M$.

2) Merge iteratively the most similar two groups
3) Repeat Step 2 until all the data are merged into a single cluster
4) Construct the clusters of messages: $S(t_\alpha, t_\beta) \geq \sigma$

In general, event logs occurred due to the same cause are created simultaneously, so correlations can be identified by comparing the event log occurring time patterns. For this, this paper uses Dynamic Time Warping (DTW), an algorithm for measuring similarity between two dynamic patterns with different time lengths. Specifically, DTW is a method that calculates optimal matching between two patterns (X and Y) by distorting two sequential data's time lengths using (2).

$$D(i,j) = min \left\{ \begin{array}{c} D(i-1, j-1) \\ D(i-1, j) \\ D(i, j-1) \end{array} \right\} + (x_i - y_j)^2 \quad (2)$$

3. Experiment Results

In this paper, event logs of OpenStack (Juno version) operated by Korea Institute of Science and Technology Information (KISTI) was collected for a day and analyzed through R.

Table 1 shows the result of message-based clustering and Fig. 1 shows the result of representing groups with distance less than 15 after calculating distance between the clustered message groups through DTW by using event occurring time. As shown in Fig. 1, there are correlation among group 3, 4, and 5 and another correlation among group 6, 7, 8, and 9. Group 3, 4, and 5 are event logs occurred from Kernal of the computing node 3 due to an error in using hard disk connected to SATA. Group 6, 7, 8, and 9 are event logs occurred from Neutron-server of the control node and Neutron l3 agent of the network node due to an error in connection between two modules. What is remarkable from the experiment in this study is finding a message group interrelated to group 6. As for the event logs (group 6) occurred due to abnormal connection between Neutron server and AMQP, the OpenStack module field of log massage shown in Table 1 is presented with root, which makes it hard to infer the cause of problem. In addition, the number of events also does not help to find correlation with other groups. However, as a result of calculating DTW distances as shown in Fig. 1, it was found that group 6 has more significant correlation with group 7, 8, and 9 than other groups.

Table 1: Clustering Results

#	Message	Description
1	07:25:00.672 31762 ERROR nova.virt.libvirt.driver [-] Getting disk size of instance-0000001b [Errno 2] No such file or directory: . . .	Do not find the VM instance in compute node
2	host name not found: 3.centos.pool.ntp.org	Do not connect with NTP server in ntpd process
3	ata4: exception Emask 0x10 SAct 0x0 SErr 0x4000000 action 0xe frozen	A kernal message to report SATA HDD read or write error
4	ata4: irq_stat 0x00000040, connection status changed	A kernal message to report SATA HDD read or write error
5	SError: {CommWake DevExch}	A kernal message to report SATA HDD read or write error
6	14:34:19.728 23037 ERROR root [-] Unexpected exception occurred 61 time(s) 2015-11-17 14:34:19.728 23037 TRACE root Traceback . . .	A error message since neutron server failed to connect to AMQP server. This message is reported periodically.
7	15:26:00.217 12870 ERROR neutron.common.legacy [-] Skipping unknown group key: firewall_driver	A error message to report unknown group key in controller/network nodes
8	15:29:40.291 13378 ERROR neutron.agent.l3_agent [-] Failed synchronizing routers	A error message since neutron l3 agent failed synchronizing routers in network node.
9	15:35:30.771 13378 ERROR neutron.agent.l3_agent [-] Failed reporting state!	A error message since neutron server failed to reporting state in network node.

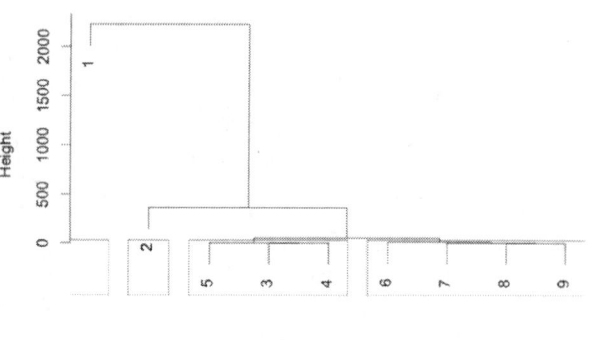

Fig. 1: Correlation among the clustered message group.

References

[1] "Openstack: Open source software for building private and public clouds." [Online]. Available: https://www.openstack.org
[2] D. J. Berndt and J. Clifford, "Using dynamic time warping to find patterns in time series." in *Proc. of KDD workshop*, vol. 10, no. 16. Seattle, WA, 1994, pp. 359–370.
[3] R. Gerhards, "Rsyslog: going up from 40k messages per second to 250k," in *Linux Kongress*, 2010.
[4] T. Pitakrat, J. Grunert, O. Kabierschke, F. Keller, and A. Van Hoorn, "A framework for system event classification and prediction by means of machine learning," in *Proc. of the 8th International Conference on Performance Evaluation Methodologies and Tools*. ICST (Institute for Computer Sciences, Social-Informatics and Telecommunications Engineering), 2014, pp. 173–180.
[5] Y. Liang, Y. Zhang, H. Xiong, and R. Sahoo, "An adaptive semantic filter for blue gene/l failure log analysis," in *Proc. of IEEE International Parallel and Distributed Processing Symposium, 2007. IPDPS 2007*. IEEE, 2007, pp. 1–8.

Int'l Conf. Grid, Cloud, & Cluster Computing | GCC'17 |

69

SESSION

LATE PAPERS - DISTRIBUTED AND CLOUD COMPUTING

Chair(s)

TBA

ISBN: 1-60132-458-8, CSREA Press ©

70

Int'l Conf. Grid, Cloud, & Cluster Computing | GCC'17 |

Evaluating Cloud Auto-Scaler Resource Allocation Planning Under High-Performance Computing Workloads

Kester Leochico and Eugene John
Department of Electrical and Computer Engineering
The University of Texas at San Antonio
San Antonio, TX

Abstract *—In this paper, we analyze the effects of changing the workload mix and lowering the average job runtime (as represented by the service rate) on the performance of three cloud auto-scalers from the literature in an effort to better model the behavior of cloud auto-scalers under high-performance computing scenarios involving long-running jobs rather than short-lived jobs as in previous studies. The simulation and analysis was carried out using the Performance Evaluation framework for Auto-Scaling (PEAS), a cloud simulator framework for modelling the performance of cloud auto-scaling algorithms using scenario theory.*

Keywords: cloud computing, auto-scaling, scenario theory

1 Introduction

Cloud computing, a high performance computing paradigm in which dynamically scalable and virtualized computing resources are provisioned to remote customers over the internet as a service on an as-needed basis [5], enables new computing resource usage cases by allowing customers to pay for access to virtually unlimited computing resources without having to pay for and maintain their own servers, allowing them to start small and scale up as-needed [3]. The key to these economic benefits is *elasticity*, the property of a computing system or application to dynamically and automatically allocate computing resources at runtime in a timely, responsive manner based on the current resource demand [2][5][11]. Elasticity enables clouds to respond to changes in the load without violating service-level agreements (SLAs) by scaling quickly in response to current demand. It also reduces the economic and environmental costs of acquiring and using computing resources by only provisioning what is needed to satisfy SLAs [3].

Because this is a very difficult task to handle properly when done manually, the task of managing elasticity is typically assigned to cloud auto-scalers. Cloud auto-scalers are subsystems within a cloud that decide how many computing resources to provision in response to current/future demand [11]. However, the current state of the art with respect to auto-scaler evaluation is immature, due to a lack of consistent benchmarking metrics [5]; a lack of formal, standard

evaluation methodologies for auto-scaling algorithms [5]; and the use of only a few short workloads to characterize auto-scaler behavior in much of the literature [1].

One proposed solution to the issues facing cloud auto-scaling evaluation is the Performance Evaluation framework for Auto-Scaling (PEAS), first proposed in [1], which aims to address the aforementioned issues with the current state-of-the-art in cloud auto-scaler performance evaluation by providing a formalized and mathematically rigorous methodology for providing probabilistic guarantees on the goodness of an auto-scaler's performance based on its distance from the ideal capacity outlay. PEAS achieves these aims in part by running as many as hundreds of workload traces to account for the effects of the workload profile on auto-scaler behavior.

In this paper, we explore the effects of changing the workload mix as well as the service rate used in the experiment (which affects how quickly/slowly jobs are processed in the simulation). Our goal is to consider how the auto-scaling algorithms described in [1] perform in terms of their ability to accurately match computing resources (in the form of virtual machines) to current demand (in the form of incoming requests) under alternate scenarios. Specifically, [1] only considered the performance of cloud auto-scaling algorithms when running under conditions that modeled a web server deployment. However, the results that the PEAS framework provides only hold if the conditions experienced in real world usage are similar to the workload mixes used in simulation. In practice, cloud computing systems can run a wide variety of workload sets, such as scientific computing workloads and data warehousing [8], and this paper aims to broaden the original experiments by considering the effects of using alternate workload sources as well as lowering the service rate of the virtual machines (VMs) used in the simulation to more closely model the job runtimes used in the aforementioned traces.

The rest of this paper is organized as follows: Section 2 provides the requisite background information on the PEAS algorithm, the underlying queuing models and principles behind it, and the auto-scalers and used in the experiment. Section 3 describes the research methodology used for the experiment, including the simulation parameters, workloads,

ISBN: 1-60132-458-8, CSREA Press ©

distance metrics, and tools involved. Section 4 presents and evaluates the results. Section 5 presents the conclusions of the study.

2   Background Information

2.1   PEAS

PEAS is a framework for providing probabilistic guarantees on auto-scaler performance. It is based on scenario theory, a technique for providing approximate solutions to chance-constrained optimization problems in which instead of solving for an exact solution to a Chance-Constrained Optimization Problem (CCP) (which is NP-hard), one can solve for the best solution under the constraint that the probability that the actual value is less than or equal to that solution is greater than or equal to $1- \epsilon$, where ϵ is the probability that the actual distance value will exceed that of the calculated solution [1].

2.1.1   Underlying Queuing Model

In order to develop the CCP, [1] models the cloud infrastructure as a G/G/N stable queue with a variable number of servers N (which represent VMs) operating in discrete time $k \in \mathbb{N}$ as shown in Figure 1. An elasticity controller attempts to match the current number of servers y(k) such that it satisfies the resource demand brought about by the incoming number of requests $\lambda(k)$, the number of queued requests that have yet to be serviced q(k), the average service rate per server (in number of requests per time unit) r_{app}, and the required capacity to service long-running requests that require more than 1 time unit to complete C_{lrr}. The ideal number of servers required to meet all currently running requests $y°(k)$ can be modeled by the following equation:

$$y°(k) = \left\lceil \frac{\lambda(k)+q(k)}{r_{app}} \right\rceil + C_{lrr}(k) \qquad (1)$$

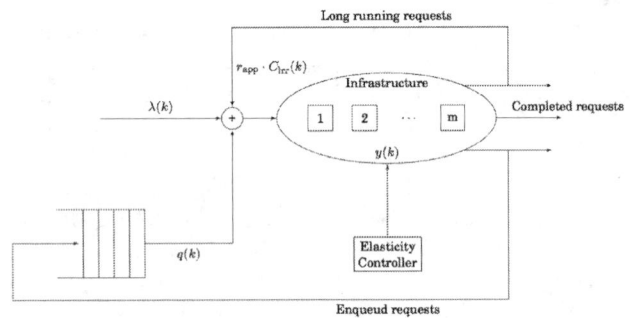

Figure 1: PEAS Queuing Model [1]

2.2   Formulation of the CCP

[1] formulates the CCP for evaluating the goodness of an auto-scaler in PEAS in terms of the following conditions:

$$\text{CCP: } \min_{\rho} \rho$$

subject to: $P\{d_{\mathcal{T}}(y, y°) \leq \rho\} \geq 1 - \epsilon, \qquad (2)$

where ρ is the probabilistic solution to the CCP and $d_{\mathcal{T}}(y, y°)$ is a distance function that represents the difference in behavior between the time series representing the actual capacity y and ideal capacity $y°$. This distance function is used as the performance metric to be considered by the PEAS algorithm, and any distance function that takes in those two inputs can be used.

2.3   Application of Scenario Theory

To solve for the aforementioned CCP, PEAS runs N experiments using N different time series, each of which represents a different representation of the stochastic input, in order to generate the time series traces $y^{(i)}$ and $y°^{(i)}$ for each experiment before generating the distance values, filtering out the κ largest distance values from the set, and returning the largest remaining value in the set. The exact process for doing so is as follows [1]:

1. Get N different time series $\lambda^{(i)}(k)$, $k = 1, 2, ..., |\mathcal{T}|$, $i = 1, 2, ..., N$ to use with the auto-scaling algorithms and let $\kappa = \lfloor \eta N \rfloor$.

2. Run the auto-scaling algorithms against each time series to generate y(k) and $y°(k)$ for each time series.

3. Compute the distance values $\hat{\rho}^{(i)} := d_{\mathcal{T}}(y^{(i)}, y°^{(i)})$ for each time series i = 1, 2, ..., N.

4. Determine the indices in the set of all input time series $(\{h_1, h_2, ..., h_\kappa\} \subset \{1, 2, ..., N\})$ of the κ largest values of the set of all distance values $\{\hat{\rho}^{(i)}, i = 1, 2, ..., N\}$

5. Return the largest value of $\hat{\rho}^{(i)}$ from the set of indices that are not in the κ largest values of the distance values set ($\hat{\rho}^* = \max_{i \in \{1, 2, ..., N\} \setminus \{h_1, h_2, ..., h_\kappa\}} \hat{\rho}^{(i)}$)

The number of experiments N and the number of results to disregard κ are in turn affected by the empirical violation parameter η and the confidence parameter β. κ is set by the following equation [1]:

$$\kappa = \lfloor \eta N \rfloor \qquad (3)$$

β, in turn, is used as part of solving the following theorem along with η to produce a value for N [1]:

If N is such that

$$\sum_{i=0}^{\lfloor \eta N \rfloor} \binom{N}{i} \epsilon^i (1 - \epsilon)^{N-i} \leq 1 - \beta,$$

ISBN: 1-60132-458-8, CSREA Press ©

Then the solution to the PEAS algorithm satisfies the restriction

$$\mathbb{P}\{d_{\mathcal{T}}(y, y^\circ) \leq \hat{\rho}^*\} \geq 1 - \epsilon \qquad (4)$$

The following guidelines hold when choosing values of β, η, and ϵ [1]:

- Increased η tends to result in increased N, as N scales as $\frac{1}{\epsilon - \eta}$, so the value of η depends on the desired value of N.

- β controls the probability that the size of the violation set will be larger than ϵ. Since the value of N is logarithmically proportional to $\frac{1}{\beta}$, β can be set as low as 10^{-10} without a significant increase in N.

- ϵ has a significant impact on the number of time series to run the algorithm with.

3   Research Methodology

3.1   Simulation Parameters

The experiments that are the subject of this paper reuse the original parameters from [1] where feasible. In particular, the following simulation parameters are used for the PEAS algorithm:

- $\eta = 0.01$

- $\epsilon = 0.05$

- $\beta = 10^{-10}$

- N = 796

- $\kappa = \lfloor \eta N \rfloor = 7$

- Time unit length = 1 minute

The main difference lies in the average service rate r_{app} (which is set to 9.075×10^{-4} requests/second = 5.445×10^{-2} requests/minute) which was derived by taking the inverse of the average runtime of each job in the Google Cluster traces [15]). Using a lower service rate allows us to better model the types of HPC workloads that are prevalent in the newer workload mixes that have been introduced in this experiment, as HPC workloads tend to have much longer per-job runtimes than the web requests that were modeled in [1] ([1] cites a service rate of 22 requests/sec). A custom Python script was used to run the PEAS post-simulation analysis algorithm described earlier.

3.2   Workloads Used

In order to test the effects of workload mix on the performance of each auto-scaler, three sets of workload traces of request rates were used. Except for the Wikipedia traces, each trace was converted to the PEAS simulator format by taking the number of jobs that were submitted during each minute-long period of the trace. The additional traces are as follows:

- *ATLAS*: The ATLAS workload set is a set of 796 minute-by-minute traces derived from Standard Workload Format (SWF) traces that were created by the workload generator described in [9]. This workload generator uses a data model derived from the workload behavior of high-performance scientific computing jobs that were run on the Nordic Data Grid Facility (NDGF) as a part of the ATLAS project at the European Organization for Nuclear Research (CERN).

- *Production:* The Production workload set is a set of 796 minute-by-minute parallel computing workload traces that were derived from various real cluster and grid computing workload traces, each of which is 3.6 weeks long. They are intended to represent typical HPC and cloud computing workloads. They include every cleaned SWF workload trace as of 2016 at the Parallel Workloads Archive [6], six grid workload traces in Grid Workload Format (GWF) from the Grid Workload Archives [7], the Google cluster traces [15], scientific computing workload traces from the CERIT Scientific Cloud [10], Hadoop traces from the OpenCloud research cluster at Carnegie Mellon University [13], and a workload trace obtained from a five month long trace at the Zewura cluster that were provided by the Czech National Grid Infrastructure MetaCentrum [10].

- *Wikipedia:* The Wikipedia workload set is a set of 796 hourly workload traces obtained from publicly available workload traces hosted by the Wikipedia foundation and used in [1]. It was generously provided by the original authors. The hourly request rates in the traces were scaled down to per-minute rates by dividing each entry by 60.

3.3   Auto-scalers Used

The experiments described in this paper use the following auto-scaler simulation code [1]. All auto-scaler algorithms are used with the default parameters provided by the simulation code, and are briefly described as follows:

- *React* [4]: *React* is a simple reactive dynamic scaling algorithm that uses threshold-based auto-scaling to add/remove VMs. It is one of the simplest scaling algorithms used in [1], and also the one that generated the best results.

- *Hist* [14]: *Hist* uses a histogram-based predictive technique that uses histograms of historical arrival rates to determine the number of resources to provision per hour. It also uses reactive provisioning to correct for prediction errors.

- *Adapt* [2]: *Adapt* adjusts the number of VMs based on both monitored load changes and predicted load changes. Predictions are based on the rate of change of the workload, and aims to adapt to sudden load changes while preventing premature resource release.

3.4   Distance Formulas Used

The following distance formulas [1] are listed as follows with a brief description. It should be noted that as these are all representing the distance between a desired value and the actual value, the lower the distance value the better:

- *Normalized Distance*: The normalized distance penalizes under-provisioning and over-provisioning identically. It uses the squared 2-norm of the difference vector $\sum_{k \in \mathcal{T}} \|y^\circ(k) - y(k)\|^2$. To account for the difference in lengths between each time series, the normalization term $\frac{1}{|\mathcal{T}|}$ is introduced. It is represented by the following equation:

$$d_{\mathcal{T}}^{norm}(y, y^\circ) = \frac{1}{|\mathcal{T}|} \sum_{k \in \mathcal{T}} \|y^\circ(k) - y(k)\|^2 \quad (5)$$

- *Modified Hausdorff Distance*: This distance metric is a modified Hausdorff distance that can account for the maximum discrepancy between the ideal and actual behavior and the probability that y will enter some set within the time horizon $\mathcal{T}$. It is represented by the following equation:

$$d_{\mathcal{T}}^{sup}(y, y^\circ) = \sup_{k \in \mathcal{T}} \|y^\circ(k) - y(k)\| \quad (6)$$

- *Over/Under-Provisioning*: These distance metrics account for the degree of over- and under-provisioning for a given auto-scaler, and are represented by the following equations:

$$d_{\mathcal{T}}^{over}(y, y^\circ) = \sup_{k \in \mathcal{T}} \|\max\{y(k) - y^\circ(k), 0\}\| \quad (7)$$

$$d_{\mathcal{T}}^{under}(y, y^\circ) = \sup_{k \in \mathcal{T}} \|\max\{y^\circ(k) - y(k), 0\}\| \quad (8)$$

- *OverT/UnderT*: The OverT and UnderT metrics [1] are a modification of the over/under provisioning metrics that measures the average over- and under-

provisioning in a time unit for a given auto-scaler, and are represented by the following equations:

$$d_{\mathcal{T}}^{overT}(y, y^\circ) = \frac{1}{|\mathcal{T}|} \sup_{k \in \mathcal{T}} \|\max\{y(k) - y^\circ(k), 0\}\| \Delta k \quad (9)$$

$$d_{\mathcal{T}}^{underT}(y, y^\circ) = \frac{1}{|\mathcal{T}|} \sup_{k \in \mathcal{T}} \|\max\{y^\circ(k) - y(k), 0\}\| \Delta k, \quad (10)$$

where Δk is the number of time units between auto-scaler algorithm interventions and is set to 1 for the purposes of this simulation.

- *Adapted Auto-Scaling Demand Index (ADI):* The ADI [12] is a measure representing the degree to which the auto-scaler is outside a given bound of acceptable utilization levels as represented by the parameters L and U, representing the lower and upper bound of acceptable utilization levels respectively. It is, in effect, a measure of the degree of over- and under-utilization. A time-normalized version of ADI [1] can be represented by the following equations:

$$u(k) = \frac{y(k)}{y^\circ(k)} \quad (11)$$

$$\sigma(k) = \begin{cases} L - u(k) & \text{if } u(k) \leq L, \\ u(k) - U & \text{if } u(k) \geq U, \\ 0 & \text{otherwise.} \end{cases} \quad (12)$$

$$\sigma = \sum_{k \in \mathcal{T}} \sigma(k) \quad (13)$$

$$\sigma_{\mathcal{T}} = \frac{\sigma}{|\mathcal{T}|} \quad (14)$$

Because traces where no VMs are required to satisfy current demands ($y^\circ(k) = 0$) at some point in the trace can result in divide-by-zero errors with the original ADI algorithm, a modified version of the time-normalized ADI algorithm is used in which $u(k) = \frac{y(k)+1}{y^\circ(k)+1}$ in order to consider the degree of over- and under-utilization even when no VMs are required. We refer to this as the *zero-corrected ADI* metric in the rest of this paper.

4   Results

4.1   Normalized Distance

Table 1 and Figure 2 show the solutions to the CCP for the normalized distance function described in (5) for each auto-scaling algorithm and workload set. The *Hist* algorithm shows the best overall ability to minimize allocation errors under the Wikipedia and Production workload mixes, while the *Adapt* algorithm provides the best performance under the ATLAS workload and the second-best performance under the other two workloads.

Table 1: Normalized distance

Workload Set	React	Hist	Adapt
ATLAS	6.890E+38	5.880E+16	**9.500E+12**
Wikipedia	6.654E+57	**5.340E+23**	1.564E+24
Production	3.959E+54	**1.032E+21**	8.941E+23

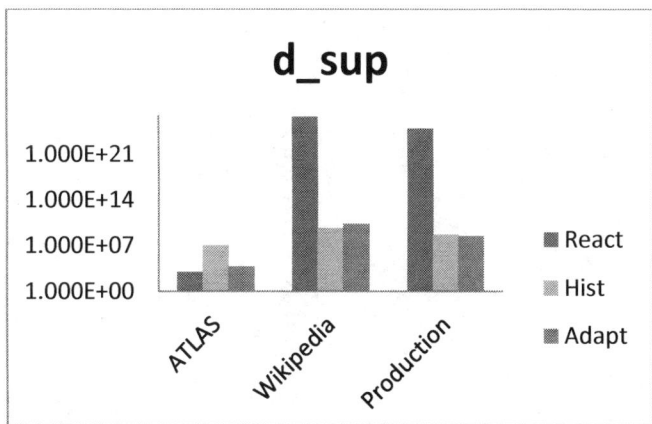

Figure 3: Results of the scenario approach with the modified Hausdorff distance

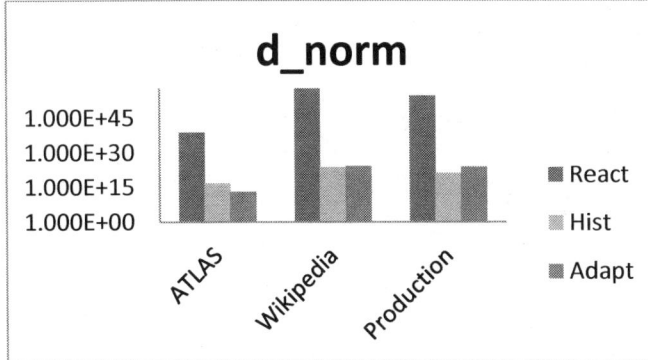

Figure 2: Results of the scenario approach with the normalized distance

4.2 Modified Hausdorff Distance

Table 2 and Figure 3 show the solutions to the CCP for the normalized distance function described in (5) for each auto-scaling algorithm and workload set. The *Adapt* algorithm shows the best overall performance with the Production workload set, while the *Hist* algorithm does the best job of minimizing allocation errors under the Wikipedia workload set and the *React* algorithm does the best job under the ATLAS workload set.

Table 2: Modified Hausdorff Distance

Workload Set	React	Hist	Adapt
ATLAS	**8.690E+02**	1.111E+07	6.582E+03
Wikipedia	5.518E+26	**4.286E+09**	2.185E+10
Production	8.338E+24	4.713E+08	**2.807E+08**

4.3 Over/Under-Provisioning

Table 3 and Figure 4 show the solutions to the CCP for the over-provisioning metric, while Table 4 and Figure 5 show the solutions to the CCP for the under-provisioning metric. While the *Hist* algorithm does the best overall job of minimizing VM over-allocation while being the second-best overall at minimizing under-allocation, the *Adapt* algorithm does a better overall job of minimizing under-allocation while having the second-best overall performance at minimizing under-allocation. The *React* algorithm, by contrast, displayed poor overall performance under both metrics.

Table 3: Over-provisioning

Workload Set	React	Hist	Adapt
ATLAS	4.779E+19	**2.470E+02**	2.574E+08
Wikipedia	4.334E+29	**4.900E+01**	2.783E+14
Production	1.014E+28	**1.720E+03**	1.801E+14

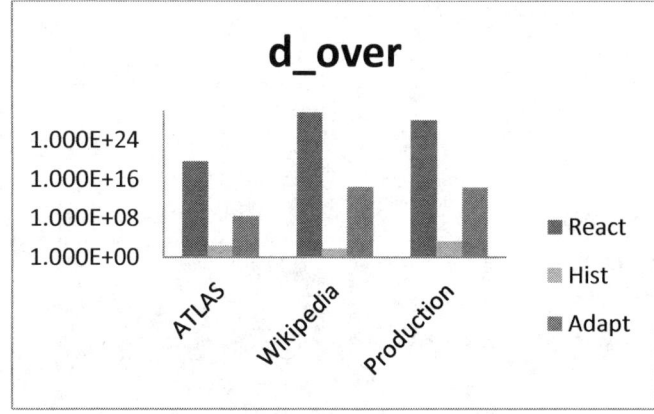

Figure 4: Results of the scenario approach with the over-provisioning metric

ISBN: 1-60132-458-8, CSREA Press ©

Table 4: Under-provisioning

Workload Set	React	Hist	Adapt
ATLAS	1.612E+21	1.241E+10	**2.988E+07**
Wikipedia	1.347E+31	1.001E+14	**8.914E+11**
Production	3.152E+29	4.977E+12	**1.666E+11**

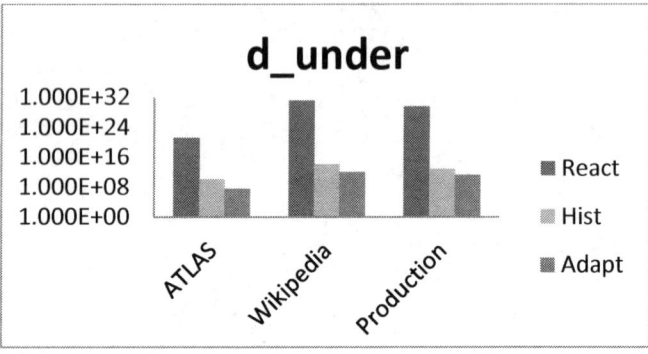

Figure 5: Results of the scenario approach with the under-provisioning metric

Table 6: UnderT

Workload Set	React	Hist	Adapt
ATLAS	6.874E+38	5.880E+16	**1.643E+11**
Wikipedia	6.644E+57	5.340E+23	**3.724E+19**
Production	3.953E+54	1.032E+21	**7.950E+17**

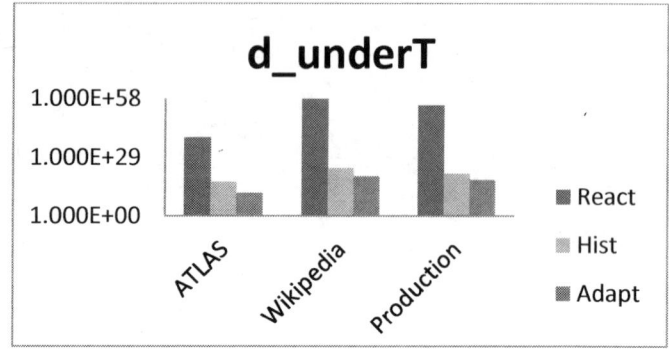

Figure 7: Results of the scenario approach with the UnderT metric

4.4   OverT/UnderT

Table 5 and Figure 6 show the solutions to the CCP for the OverT metric, while Table 6 and Figure 7 show the solutions to the CCP for the UnderT metric. Similar behavior was exhibited across all auto-scalers and workload sets between OverT/UnderT and the over-provisioning/under-provisioning metrics respectively.

Table 5: OverT

Workload Set	React	Hist	Adapt
ATLAS	4.779E+19	**2.470E+02**	2.574E+08
Wikipedia	4.334E+29	**4.900E+01**	2.783E+14
Production	1.014E+28	**1.720E+03**	1.801E+14

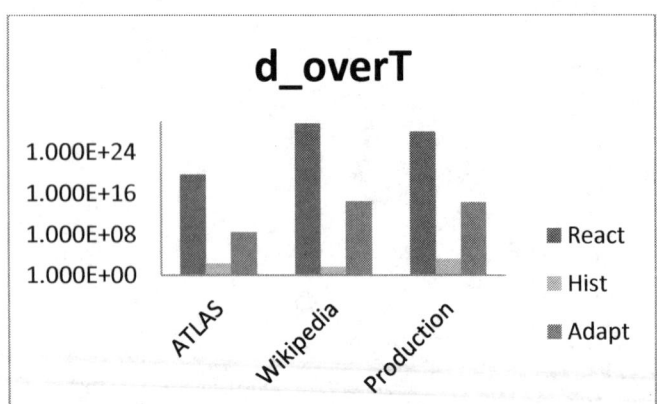

Figure 6: Results of the scenario approach with the OverT metric

4.5   ADI

Table 7 and Figure 8 show the CCP solutions for the zero-corrected ADI. Across all workload sets, the *React* algorithm demonstrates the best ability to closely track the allocation targets, although the *Hist* algorithm is second-best at tracking allocation targets. The *Adapt* algorithm demonstrates the worst overall performance.

Table 7: ADI (Zero-corrected)

Workload Set	React	Hist	Adapt
ATLAS	**3.053E-01**	8.997E-01	1.497E+03
Wikipedia	**3.047E-01**	9.000E-01	4.044E+04
Production	**3.050E-01**	9.000E-01	4.586E+06

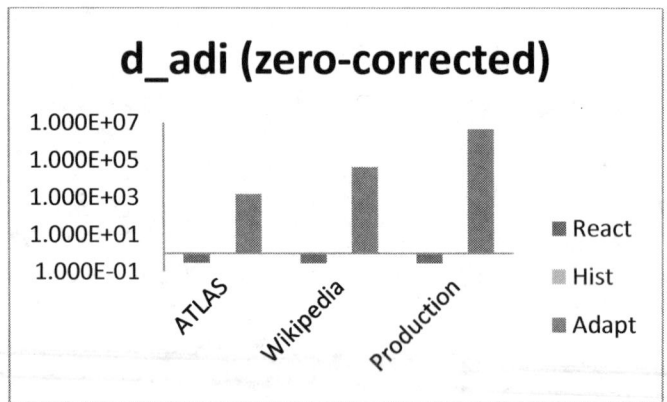

Figure 8: Results of the scenario approach with the zero-corrected ADI metric

ISBN: 1-60132-458-8, CSREA Press ©

5 Conclusions

In this paper, we studied the effects of modifying the workload mix and job runtimes (as represented by the service rate) on the accuracy of cloud resource allocation planning. The divergent results observed in these experiments from [1] illustrates the importance of tailoring auto-scaling strategies to the workloads and performance characteristics at hand. Whereas [1] demonstrated that the *React* algorithm displayed better performance across most of the metrics used in this study for the Wikipedia workload set, our results demonstrate that for cases where the service rate and job runtimes are significantly lower, the *Hist* and *Adapt* algorithms do a better overall job of minimizing allocation errors and minimizing the length of periods of over- and under-allocation across all metrics except for ADI, where the *React* algorithm excels at tracking the required allocation. As a next step towards extending the work covered in this study, more work needs to be done to characterize each of the workload sets in order to figure out the effects of specific workload characteristics on auto-scaler behavior.

6 Acknowledgment

The authors of this paper would like to thank Ahmed Ali-Eldin Hassan from Umeå University for providing the original source code for the Python-based event simulator from [1], source code for the auto-scaling algorithms used in this paper, and the Wikipedia web traces. This paper would not be possible without his support and advice.

7 References

[1] A. Ali-Eldin Hassan, "Workload characterization, controller design and performance evaluation for cloud capacity autoscaling," Umeå University, 2015.

[2] A. Ali-Eldin, J. Tordsson, and E. Elmroth, "An adaptive hybrid elasticity controller for cloud infrastructures," in 2012 IEEE Network Operations and Management Symposium, 2012, pp. 204–212.

[3] M. Armbrust, I. Stoica, M. Zaharia, A. Fox, R. Griffith, A. D. Joseph, R. Katz, A. Konwinski, G. Lee, D. Patterson, and A. Rabkin, "A view of cloud computing," Commun. ACM, vol. 53, no. 4, p. 50, Apr. 2010.

[4] T. C. Chieu, A. Mohindra, A. A. Karve, and A. Segal, "Dynamic Scaling of Web Applications in a Virtualized Cloud Computing Environment," in 2009 IEEE International Conference on e-Business Engineering, 2009, pp. 281–286.

[5] E. F. Coutinho, F. R. de Carvalho Sousa, P. A. L. Rego, D. G. Gomes, and J. N. de Souza, "Elasticity in cloud computing: a survey," Ann. Telecommun. - Ann. des télécommunications, vol. 70, no. 7–8, pp. 289–309, Aug. 2015.

[6] D. Feitelson, "Logs of Real Parallel Workloads from Production Systems," 2015. [Online]. Available: http://www.cs.huji.ac.il/labs/parallel/workload/logs.html.

[7] "The Grid Workloads Archive." [Online]. Available: http://gwa.ewi.tudelft.nl/.

[8] IBM, "Get more out of cloud with a structured workload analysis," no. October, 2011.

[9] D. Karpenko, R. Vitenberg, and A. L. Read, "ATLAS grid workload on NDGF resources: Analysis, modeling, and workload generation," Futur. Gener. Comput. Syst., vol. 47, pp. 31–47, Jun. 2015.

[10] D. Klusáček, "Dalibor Klusáček - Home Page," 2016. [Online]. Available: http://www.fi.muni.cz/~xklusac/index.php?page=meta2009.

[11] T. Lorido-Botran, J. Miguel-Alonso, and J. A. Lozano, "A Review of Auto-scaling Techniques for Elastic Applications in Cloud Environments," J. Grid Comput., vol. 12, no. 4, pp. 559–592, Dec. 2014.

[12] M. A. S. Netto, C. Cardonha, R. L. F. Cunha, and M. D. Assuncao, "Evaluating Auto-scaling Strategies for Cloud Computing Environments," in 2014 IEEE 22nd International Symposium on Modelling, Analysis & Simulation of Computer and Telecommunication Systems, 2014, pp. 187–196.

[13] K. Ren, "OpenCloud Hadoop cluster trace." [Online]. Available: http://ftp.pdl.cmu.edu/pub/datasets/hla/.

[14] B. Urgaonkar, P. Shenoy, A. Chandra, and P. Goyal, "Dynamic Provisioning of Multi-tier Internet Applications," in Second International Conference on Autonomic Computing (ICAC'05), 2005, pp. 217–228.

[15] J. Wilkes, "More Google cluster data," Nov-2011. [Online]. Available: http://googleresearch.blogspot.com/2011/11/more-google-cluster-data.html.

A Review of Electric Vehicle Charging Impact on Power Grid

Azhar Ul-Haq, Saif ullah Awan

College of Electrical and Mechanical Engineering, National University of Sciences and Technology, Islamabad, Pakistan

Email: azhar.ulhaq@ceme.nust.edu.pk

Abstract—In view of increasing popularization of electric vehicles (EVs) in transportation system, it has become necessary to carry out comprehensive review of EVs charging impact on the power system along with its positive impact in terms of cost-benefits and environment. Voltage drop, unbalance, and harmonic distortion have been among the main power quality concerns due to largely expected penetration of electric vehicles in the system. Thus, these has been reviewed and analyzed in this paper. A cost-benefit analysis is carried out for different penetration levels of EVs. Additionally, a substantial focus is given to compute the overloading of transformer, cable, and increased energy losses that appear after integration of single-phase electric vehicle charging load in a distribution network. The obtained results may serve as a guiding parameters for future network reinforcements.

Index Terms—Electric vehicles, voltage drop, voltage unbalance, harmonic distortion, energy losses

I. INTRODUCTION

Popularization of EVs is becoming high rather than discussing their negative impact on electrical distribution system and it is assumed that the distribution system is capable enough to support EVs' load [1], and it is not true in real. As the most likely point for charging an EV is home, so a large penetration of e-vehicles may overburden the present power infrastructure with a rise of power quality issues which may be detrimental to a sustainable power infrastructure. However, recently, some researchers have discussed the limitations of distribution network capacity for EV charging [2], [3]. Several research papers are focused to assess the EVs' impact on power grid [4], [5] and other studies about EVs' impact on the power distribution system are described in [6], [7]. Large-scale integration of EVs is likely to put certain impact on the power system infrastructure, mainly on LV power distribution system [8]. As EV load is directly interfaced with the distribution network so it may affect the power system multifariously. Impact of EV charging load on the operation of power distribution system can be broadly considered in terms of technical concerns and economic issues. In technical context, mostly loads connected to the system need an appropriate level of power quality and such loads may fail to function properly in case of variations in the fundamental parameters of power system i.e. voltage, frequency and or current. Consequently, some components e.g. transformers and motors may face reduced lifespan. Quantity of power quality indices is restricted by a number of relevant standards. Generally, a specific system is considered and studied, for evaluation of power quality index, that is aimed at identifying potential problems and causes

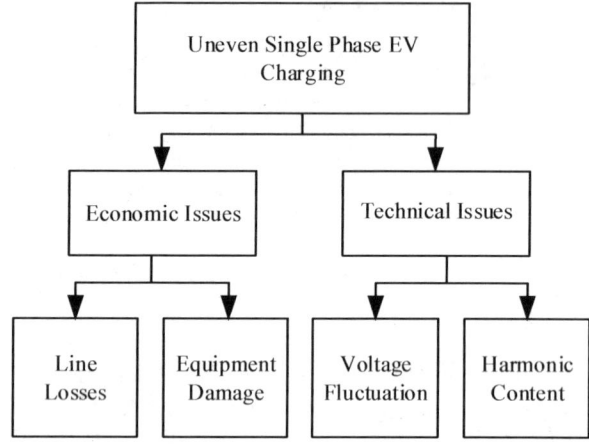

Figure 1. Concerns related to EV charging load

of the issues in the system because power quality depends on various factors ranging from power generation site to the point of ultimate consumption. Thus, envisaged EVs´ impact on power distribution system includes over-rated power flow in distribution lines, overloading of transformers, harmonic distortion, voltage unbalance and etc [9]. Additionally, EVs are characterized as a single-phase electrical load in a 3-phase distribution system and it's well known fact that presence of large single phase loads and their uneven distribution on each phase causes voltage unbalance in the system.

This presented paper is arranged as: technical and economic impact of EVs is explained in Sec. II, vulnerability of distribution network is described in Sec. III. Formulation of voltage drop, voltage unbalance and harmonic distortion is presented in Sec. IV. A business model of EVs charging is briefed in Sec. V. Transformer and cable overloading is detailed in Sec. VI, and Sec. VII contains energy losses. The paper is concluded in Sec. VIII.

II. TECHNICAL AND ECONOMIC IMPACT OF EVS

Large-scale integration of EVs put certain impact on power system infrastructure, mainly on LV power distribution system. As EV load is directly interfaced with the distribution network for former´s charging. EVs may affect the system multifariously that can broadly be classified into technical and economic concerns as illustrated in Fig. 1.

A. Economic Concerns

EV battery chargers are equipped with power electronic components for recharging EVs and former are characterized as non-linear loads or distorting loads which introduce harmonics in the system. Importantly, presence of voltage unbalance in the system induces non-characteristic triplet current harmonics e.g. 3rd and 9th harmonics adding them with characteristic harmonics of power converters. In power electronic interfaced loads, a small increase in voltage unbalance may cause input current to become significantly unbalanced that causes change its waveform into single-pulse from a double-pulse due to asymmetrical behavior of power electronic elements. Excessive flow of phase currents in a three phase system due to the voltage unbalance may cause circuits of overload-protection to trip. As harmonic injection in the system causes an increase in phase currents so it leads to increased lines losses and overloading of cables. Harmonic contamination induced by VU in the distribution network alters reactive power circulation abnormally and voltage regulation problems that badly affects working efficiency of distribution transformer and results in the decreased life of machines. Where, increased line losses, de-rating of induction machines, decreased efficiency and reduced life of power equipment are described as an economic concern for DSOs. Thus VU caused by uneven single phase load of EVs is quite harmful to economy of a distribution network.

B. Technical Concerns

In the technical context, a power quality problem can be described as manifestation of any violations in the operating range of voltage, frequency or current of the power system that results in malfunctioning of equipment,. Since a decade, power quality has been gaining due attention because of to its effects on components in the system. Mostly, loads need an appropriate level of power quality and such loads may fail to function properly in case of variations in the fundamental parameters of power system i.e. voltage, frequency and or current and consequently, some of components e.g. transformers and motors may face reduced lifespan. Thus, it is quite important to assess power quality index including, voltage unbalances, frequency variations, harmonic content, voltage drop and etc. Quantity of power quality indices is restricted by a number of international standards. Generally, a specific system is considered and studied, for evaluation of any power quality index, that is aimed at identifying potential problems and causes of the issue in the system. Power quality depends on various factors ranging from power generation site to the point of ultimate consumption and the elements connected to it.

III. VULNERABILITY OF DISTRIBUTION NETWORK

The impact of connection of EV load on low-voltage distribution system is of great concern because of latter's specific characteristics. As an LV distribution system is characterized with varying loads, unbalanced phase voltages, higher value of resistances on its branches, low reactance values, i.e. small ratio of X/R with radial structure as compared to medium

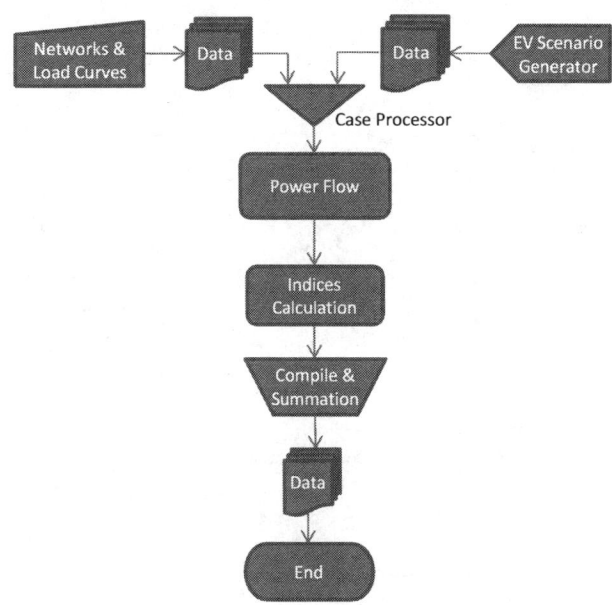

Figure 2. Flow-Chart: EV impact analysis on LV grid

voltage (MV) networks so it exhibits power quality problems. As a fact of matter low voltage networks are termed as the weaker portion of electrical power system. It implies that in case of even small variation in demand and supply could arouse worse effects in the power distribution system. It can be explained in view of the fact that the LV distribution lines have limited capacity of the connected equipment with impedance from HV/MV lines which results in problematic power supply with large impedance.

Taking this into account, the LV distribution system is expected to suffer a significant impact following a future scenario with large scale EV integration which can affect system performance. In this context, an EV impact analysis for LV distribution grids is required to identify the impact of EV charging connection to the systems while providing with the means to deal with them. In order to analyze the impact of EVs' charging connection on the operation of LV distribution grids, a steady-state tool should be used. The tool should be able to take into account the specific characteristics of LV distribution systems with EV integration, especially the fact that LV grids are generally unbalanced and, more importantly, it must be able to model and implement the EV demand for different scenarios. For this reason, a specific tool is adopted in order to perform the following required tasks:

- Define EV demand, charging method and mobility
- Run an LV three-phase power flow routine
- Verify the main technical constraints of the system (such as system losses, voltage profiles)
- Provide supply quality and system performance parameters and indexes calculation (namely voltage imbalances and load imbalances)
- Compile the results from different scenarios.

The entire process is shown in the flow chart in Fig. 2 and the description is explained below.

ISBN: 1-60132-458-8, CSREA Press ©

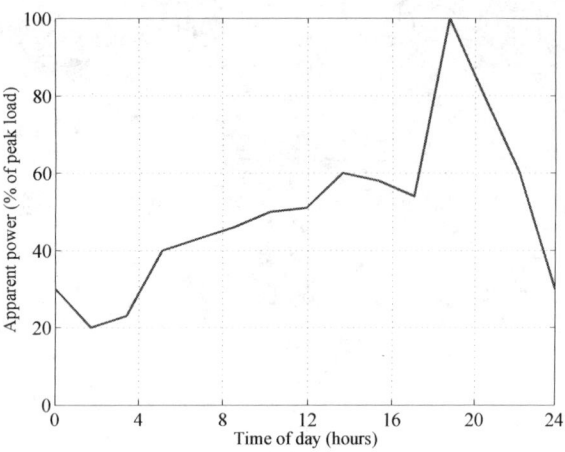

Figure 3. Daily loading on a distribution network ([12])

A load flow routine was worked out in order to be capable of dealing with the specificity of LV distribution networks, mainly the existence of three unbalanced phases plus a neutral conductor and lines with a low X/R ratio. This routine will help analyze the steady state performance of an LV network and dealing with single-phase loads and different micro-generation technologies. A first version of the algorithm was developed in [10] as a microgrid analysis tool, and extended to four-wire systems in [11] being used for three-phase radial distribution network. Although designed for radial distribution networks, it may be adapted for meshed networks. However, this is no obstacle since the test-networks to be used are typical LV distribution grids with a radial structure.

IV. FORMULATION OF VOLTAGE DROP, UNBALANCE AND HARMONIC DISTORTION

Definition of voltage drop given by EN 50160 is: "decrease in voltage due to load variation". Voltage drop is one of the most likely problems that may be observed in case of large scale EV penetration in the distribution network. When a light load is connected, the system could feed a large amount of additional load within its allowed limits. Thus, a particular number of EVs can be connected to a distribution system without being subjected to the power quality problem.

To investigate the voltage drop in the distribution system, peak load hours of the feeder are considered. During this period, at the possible occurrence of maximum load on the feeder, a severe voltage drop is expected to occur. A load curve on daily basis given in [12] shows the fraction of power demand as an apparent demand of the power system as depicted in Fig. 3. The curve exhibits that the load is 30 % of the peak demand from midnight to 6 am.

Voltage drop ΔV_D from point R_k to the other end of the feeder is expressed as in Eq. (1)

$$\Delta V_D = R_k \left(n - R_k + 1 \right) \frac{\sqrt{P^2 + Q^2} z_1}{V_{nom}} \qquad (1)$$

where, z_1 is the impedance of line segments between two nodes, n is the number of nodes, P and Q represent active and reactive power and V_{nom} is the fundamental value of voltage.

A. Voltage Unbalance

Definition of voltage unbalance in this paper is taken as a ratio of negative sequence to positive sequence component in a three phase circuit. As expressed in Eq. (2).

$$Voltage\,Unbalance\,Factor(\%) = \frac{V_2}{V_1} * 100 \approx \sqrt{\frac{1 - \sqrt{3 - 6\beta}}{1 + \sqrt{3 - 6\beta}}} \qquad (2)$$

where, $\beta = \dfrac{V_{ab}^4 + V_{bc}^4 + V_{ca}^4}{\left(V_{ab}^2 + V_{bc}^2 + V_{ca}^2 \right)^2}$

Where, V_1 and V_2 are positive and negative sequence voltage components.

B. Harmonics Evaluation

Generally, harmonics originate from power electronic interfaced loads. Harmonic in the power system may cause significant problems in the form of excessive heating of AC electric machines, transformers and occurrence of resonance in the system, thus posing technical as well as economic concerns [13]. As electric vehicles are connected to the distribution system though power electronic interface so these represent an addition of non-linear load in the system. A harmonic pattern provided by any non-linear load means a specific harmonic content and its quantitative amount is expressed as total harmonic distortion.

Total current and voltage harmonic distortion in a system $(THD)_i$ $(THD)_v$ can be expressed as given in Eq. (3) and 4.

$$THD_i = \frac{\sqrt{\sum_{h=2}^{H} \left(I_k^h \right)^2}}{I_k^1} \qquad (3)$$

$$THD_v = \frac{\sqrt{\sum_{h=2}^{H} \left(V_k^h \right)^2}}{V_k^1} \qquad (4)$$

where h represents the order of harmonics, H represents highest number of harmonic, I_h is the RMS value of the h component and I_1 is the component of fundamental frequency. Typically, an EV charging is performed through power electronic converters and there has been rapid evolution of robust topologies and control schemes of power converters for the same purpose [14], [15].

C. Relevant Standards

The standards EN 56160 and IEC 61000 are considered to be the most relevant for assessment of voltage variations. EN 50160 defines that the voltage variations in a public distribution networks at consumer's terminal should not be any beyond 10% of the nominal voltage specificity. Generally, it requires that the voltage must not go beyond the limit of

±10 of the rated voltage value [16] and standard IEC 61000 also limits voltage drop up to 10% [17]. In that division, LV feeder, MV/LV transformer and cable connections are assigned voltage variations of 4%, 2.5%, and 1.5% respectively. An overall allowable limit of 9% is considered in the simulation setup instead of exactly 10%.

In view of EV integration in the system and the related harmonics effect include current harmonic content that is injected into the power grid and voltage harmonics caused by distorted current into the system. Quantitative amount of current harmonics into the power grid are defined by a number of standards.

However, in some cases the content of voltage unbalance may reach up to 3%. Another standard defined by EMC, EN 61000 limits to 2% only [18]. IEEE recommended practice allows VU of 2 or 2.5 % for some electronic equipment [13]. IEC restricts the voltage unbalance up to 1 %, otherwise motor should be derated. Standards IEC 61000 and EN 50160 are considered to meet EVs' charging requirements [19], [16].

V. BUSINESS MODEL OF EVS CHARGING

A sustainable growth of EVs in transportation system needs extensive charging facilities, up-gradation of distribution system and accumulated control approaches for their market integration. According to authors in [20], [21], we consider a case of EV charging at public point and determine the total cost of the stations including the cost of maintenance and administration and installation cost. The charging station can serve an EV charging on both slow and fast charging modes with time of charging ranges from 15 min to 12h . Its cost is 2130 € for a slow charging station of maximum power of 3.5 kW at a public lot and the cost will be 44692 € for a fast charging station of power up to 10 kW.

a) Cost Estimation: The cost for EV charging infrastructure (EV_{DCI}) can be determined (in €) as given in Eq. (5):

$$EV_{DCI} = EV_{PL}.T_{CV}.\left(C_{pp} + C_{RU} + C_{CMS} + C_{Eq.} + C_{DNE}\right) \quad (5)$$

Where, EV_{PL} is EV penetration level, T_{CV} represents the cost of conventional gasoline vehicles, C_{pp} and C_{RU} stand for charging stations cost at public parking and charging station's cost at a residential unit. C_{CMS} stands for the control cost and management software, $C_{Eq.}$ stands for the cost of equipment and C_{DNE} represents the expansion cost of the network.

The cost of ambient factors in € may be computed as expressed in Eq. (6):

$$C_{AF} = AL_{EV}\left(TC_{Em.} + TC_{cc} + TC_N\right) \quad (6)$$

TC_{AF} is the total cost of external factors, AL_{EV} represents the average life of electric vehicle, $TC_{Em.}$ is the cost of emission, TC_{cc} stands for climate change, TC_N is the cost of noise.

Table I
ACTUAL LOADING AND THE CURRENT CARRYING CAPACITY OF CABLES
OF URBAN DISTRIBUTION SYSTEM WITH EV PENETRATION OF 45 %

Node from	Node to	Cable name	Current capacity (A)	Current PL: 45 %
R1	R2	G1	395	383.5
R9	R10	G1	395	92.3
R3	R11	G3	58	46
R12	R13	G4	157	96.8
R6	R16	G3	157	148.1
R10	R18	G3	157	101.4

VI. TRANSFORMER, CABLE OVERLOADING AND ENERGY LOSSES

This section describes and illustrates the transformer, cable loading and increased energy losses that appear after integration of single phase electric vehicle charging load. As the power demand increases due to additional load of EVs, it causes to raise the current flow, so it provokes energy losses to increase. In order to evaluate the increased energy losses, a base case as a reference point is taken to quantify the impact of EV penetration levels. The reference point is taken as the network condition which supplies energy to the actual consumers within the allowed limits of voltage unbalance content, before connection of EVs on the distribution system. It has been noted that active power losses increase after connection of EVs in the system, particularly at a certain level of penetration of EVs when voltage unbalance is detected beyond its standard limit.

Besides voltage drop and voltage unbalance, it may also be important to see the effect of EVs addition in the system in terms of loading of transformer and power cables. In this section, transformer and cable loading are considered and assessed. In case of urban distribution system, current carrying capacity of the power cables according to [12] before addition of EVs and thereafter, current flow in each segment of the cable with the above mentioned penetration levels and scenarios are given in Tab. I. The rated current and actual amount of load on the transformer for the corresponding scenarios are 433A and 389A respectively. Likelihood of the overloading conditions are also mentioned. The values of all line segments are not specified but some of them are summarized here for simplicity and demonstration of the problem.

The given values in Tab. I indicate that the cable and transformer loading remain within the allowed capacity at EV penetration levels of 45 %. However, the actual flow of current could violate the capacity in case of higher penetration level. The system load corresponds to the excessive voltage drop on some nodes of the distribution system which are found near the built-in capacity. It shows that the transformer and cables operate closed to the current limits and these segments are likely to be overload with higher degree of load. Increased energy losses are shown in Fig. 4

In case of the rural distribution network, current carrying

ISBN: 1-60132-458-8, CSREA Press ©

Table II
ACTUAL LOADING AND THE CURRENT CARRYING CAPACITY OF CABLES
OF RURAL DISTRIBUTION SYSTEM WITH EV PENETRATION OF 25 %

Node from	Node to	Cable name	Current capacity (A)	Current PL: 25%
C2	C3	L1	270	171.2
C11	C12	L1	270	91.6
C4	C13	L2	145	73
C14	C15	L2	145	46.7
C20	C22	L3	110	103.5
C12	C24	L4	110	23.8

Table III
LOADING ON THE URBAN DISTRIBUTION NETWORK

Node	No. of households	Max. Load (kVA)
R11	9	16
R15	25	33
R16	48	68
R17	09	14
R18	21	45

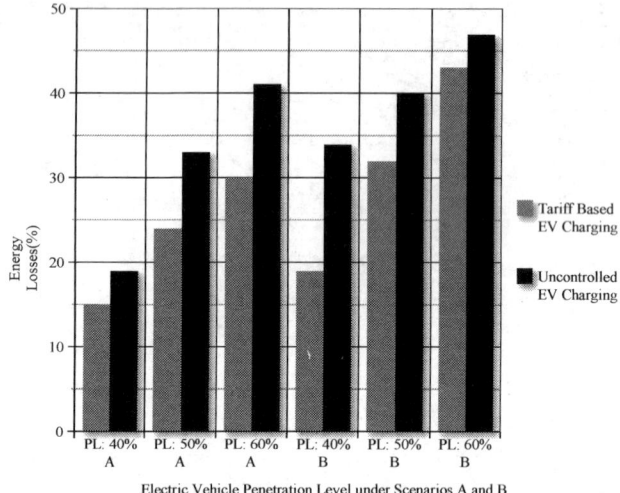

Figure 4. Increased energy losses

capacity of the overhead power cables, before addition of EVs and load and after the load of EVs are mentioned in Tab. II, where flowing current at additional load of EV penetration level of 25 % is compared with the rated current of the line segments. Regarding transformer load, there is rated current of 216.5 A and the actual flowing current is 183.4 A.

It could be observed from the recorded values, the current does not approach the rated limit under the studied case, despite the voltage drop reaches its maximum permissible limits. Thus the voltage drop stands as a dominant factor for the additional load of EV charging in the rural area. In the urban distribution network under considered scenarios, results show that the voltage drop in the system approaches its limits before overloading of conductors and transformers. Though, the cables nearer to the distribution feeder and MV/LV transformer are heavily loaded and that may face overloading with a little addition of load on the feeder. The overloading may happen explicitly of voltage loss in the system, it may occur when additional heavy load is concentrated closer to the transformer. In case of rural network, the voltage loss appears much before cable of transformer overloading are observed and it is justified with the fairly long power cables in the rural area. It is noted that the obtained results might not be applicable for all urban or rural areas. For instance, the situation may differ with diverse topologies of distribution system and cable lengths of the power lines. Thus the carried out study be considered an example for investigating the voltage drop issue the power distribution network. Additionally, this section describes and illustrates increased energy losses due to integration of single phase electric vehicle charging load. As the power demand increases due to additional load of EVs, it causes to raise the current flow, so it provokes energy losses to increase. In order to evaluate the increased energy losses, a base case as a reference point is taken to quantify the impact of EV penetration levels. The reference point is taken as the network condition which supplies energy to the actual consumers within the allowed limits of voltage unbalance content, before connection of EVs in the system as mentioned in Tab. III. It is observed that active power losses increase after connection of EVs in the system, particularly at a certain level of penetration of EVs when voltage unbalance is detected beyond its standard limit.

VII. RESULTS

Percentage of increase in the energy losses is recorded with the different EV penetration levels. Increment in the losses is

found to be a bit higher in case of uncontrolled EV charging. Whereas, adoption of tariff based charging scheme makes it possible to decrease power losses in the urban distribution system. Thus, uncontrolled charging of EVs shows worst results as it leads to high peak loads and in turn that causes higher power losses in the LV distribution system. In this study, EVs are replicated as a single phase electrical loads at a particular node. It shows its impact as an additional load on the increased current at a specific point. The flow of power algorithm is based on the iterative process presented in [11], through which node current, voltage and overloaded line segments are identified and total power losses are computed in the LV network. The result related to increased energy losses (%) due to integration of single phase electric vehicle charging load is shown in simulation section.

Increase in consumption for 24 hours is depicted in Fig. 5 for EV penetration levels of 50% and 60%. The result shown in Fig. 6 illustrates that the appeared voltage THD, recorded at different EV penetration levels, in the distribution system violates the permissible limit of 8 % in many cases. Thus, for this level of THD, it could be seen that EVs may contaminate the system by harmonic injection. For the worst scenario, the voltage harmonic distortion can reach the limits when EV penetration level is higher than 45 %.

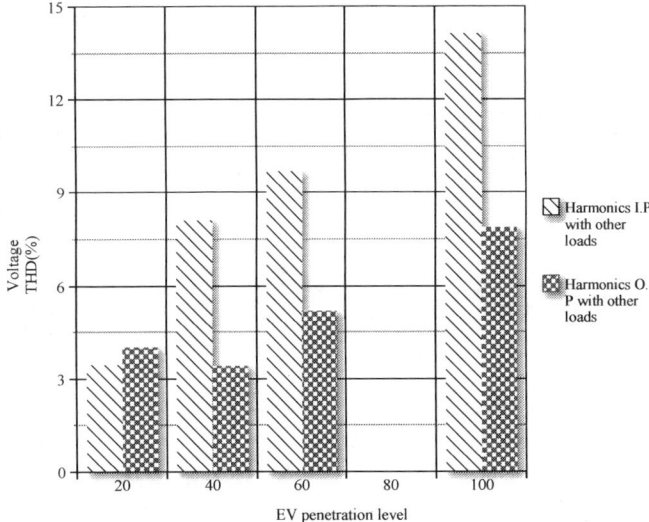

Figure 6. Voltage harmonic caused by EV charging with current THD of 17.4%

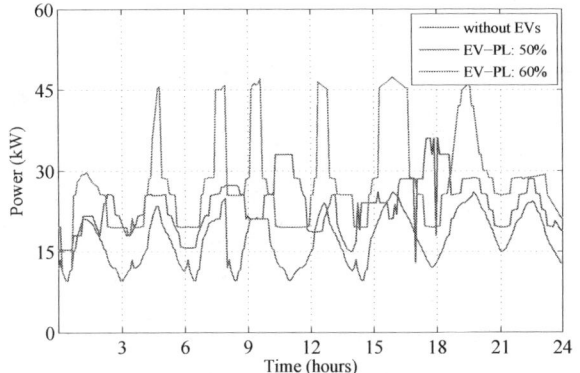

Figure 5. Rise in power consumption

VIII. CONCLUSION

It becomes a evident that a large-scale adoption of electric vehicles will substantially affect the current power system operating practices. Several quality parameters including voltage drop, unbalance, harmonic distortion, cable and transformer overloading, and increased energy losses due to additional load of EVs are formulated and quantified in this paper. It is suggested that the network reinforcement for EVs may be designed based on the presented violating figures of power quality indices. It is important to visualize that there might be a situation when the systems does not remain capable of supporting further load of EV charging because of the violation in system's operating parameters. Thus, definite up-gradation requirements must be investigated before EVs' charging load is added in the distribution system.

REFERENCES

[1] K. Clement, K. Van Reusel, and J. Driesen, "The consumption of electrical energy of plug-in hybrid electric vehicles in Belgium," *in Proc. 2nd Eur. Ele-Drive Transportation Conf.*, Brussels, May 2007.

[2] P. Richardson, D. Flynn, A. Keane, "Impact assessment of varying penetrations of electric vehicles on low voltage distribution systems," in *Proc. of IEEE Pow. and En. Soc. Gen. Meet.* Minneapolis, MN, pp. 1-6, 2010.

[3] V. Tikka, J. Lassila, J. Haakana, J. Partanen, "Case Study of the Effects of Electric Vehicle Charging on Grid Loads in an Urban Area," *in Proc. of IEEE PES Int. Conf. and Exhibition on Innovative Smart Grid Techno.*, pp. 1-7, Dec. 2011.

[4] W. Kempton and J. Tomic, "Vehicle-to-grid power fundamentals: Calculating capacity and net revenue," *J. Pow. Sources*, vol. 144, no. 1, pp. 268–279, 2005.

[5] E. Sortomme, M. M. Hindi, S.D.J MacPherson, S.S. Venkata, "Coordinated charging of PHEV to minimize distribution losses," *in IEEE Trans. Smart Grid*, vol. 2 , no. 1, pp. 198 - 205, Feb. 2011.

[6] J. A. Orr, A. E. Emanuel, D. J. Pileggi, "Current Harmonics, Voltage Distortion, and Powers Associated with Electric Vehicle Battery Chargers Distributed on the Residential Power System," *IEEE Trans. on Ind. App.*, vol. Ia-20, no. 4, pp. 727 – 734. Aug. 1984.

[7] K. Clement-Nyns, E. Haesen, and J. Driesen, "The impact of charging plug-in hybrid electric vehicles on a residential distribution grid," *IEEE Trans. on Power Syst.*, vol. 25, no. 1, pp. 371–380, Feb. 2010.

[8] Rui Shi, "The Dynamic Impacts of Electric Vehicle Integration on the Electricity Distribution Grid," " *M.Phil thesis*, Sch. of Electron. Elect. and Comp. Engg, The Univ. of Birmingham, UK, Nov. 2012.

[9] Green, C. Robert, L. Wang and M. Alam, "The impact of plug-in hybrid electric vehicles on distribution networks: A review and outlook," *Elsevier Journal of Renewable and Sustainable Energy Reviews* vol. 15, no. 1, pp. 544-553, 2011.

[10] André Guimarães Madureira, "Coordinated and Optimized Voltage Management of Distribution Networks with Multi-Microgrids," *PhD thesis*, Department of Electrical and Computer Engineering, University of Porto, Porto, July, 2010.

[11] R. M. Ciric, A. Padilha-Feltrin, L. F. Ochoa, "Power flow in four-wire distribution networks-general approach," in *IEEE Trans. Power Syst.*, vol. 18, no. 4, pp. 1283-1290, Nov. 2003.

[12] K. Strunz, N. Hatziargyriou, C. Andrieu "Benchmark Systems for Network Integration of Renewable and Distributed Energy Resources," CIGRE Task Force C6.04.02, 2013.

[13] IEEE Recommended Practices and Requirements for Harmonic Control in Electrical Power Systems, IEEE Std. 519-1992, April 1993.

[14] M. A. S. Masoum, S. Deilami, S. Islam, "Mitigation of harmonics in smart grids with high penetration of plug-in electric vehicles," *in Proc. of IEEE General Meeting of Power and Energy Society*, pp. 1-6, Jul. 2010

[15] R. Bass, R. Harley, F. Lambert, V. Rajasekaran and J. Pierce, "Residential harmonic loads and ev charging," in *Proc. of IEEE Power Engineering Society Winter Meeting*, vol. 2, pp. 803–808, Feb. 2001.

[16] EN 50160, "Voltage characteristics of electricity supplied by public distribution systems, " Sep. 2007.

[17] H. Markiewicz, A. Klajn, "Voltage Disturbances: EN 50160, Voltage characteristics of electricity supplied by public distribution systems," Leonardo Power Quality Initiative, Copper Development Association, July 2004.

[18] EPRI Power Electronics Applications Center, "Input performance of ASDs during supply voltage unbalance," Power quality testing network PQTN Brief no. 28, 1996.

[19] International Standard IEC 61000-4-30, Electromagnetic compatibility (EMC) – Part 4-30: Testing and measurement techniques – Power quality measurement methods, 2003.

[20] F. Nemry, G. Leduc, and A. Munoz, "Plug-in Hybrid and Battery Electric Vehicles." Institute for Prospective Technological Studies, Jun-2010.

[21] F. Avila and F. Gonzalez, "Conexión de vehiculos a la red electrica (V2G)." Pontificia Universidad Católica de Chile.

ISBN: 1-60132-458-8, CSREA Press ©

Author Index

Alhafdi, Maram   -   42
Awan, Saif ullah   -   78
Barnawi, Ahmed   -   42
Beranek, Marek   -   24
Budhi, Lokesh   -   3
Chou, Li-Der   -   31
Dasgupta, Ranjan   -   17
Dulimarta, Hans   -   35
Feuerlicht, George   -   24
Gennepally, Spandana   -   3
Goswami, Paromita   -   17
Hong, Tae-Young   -   65
John, Eugene   -   71
Kim, BoKyoung   -   55
Kim, Eunhye   -   67
Kim, Sung-Jun   -   65
Kim, YeongMok   -   55
Kirkman, Stephen S.   -   10
Kovar, Vladimir   -   24
Lee, Frank   -   3
Lee, Jae-Kook   -   65
Leochico, Kester   -   71
Medellin, John   -   3
Newman, Richard   -   10
Park, Ju-Won   -   67
Park, SungHoon Park   -   55
Rios, Leopoldo J.   -   49
Singha Roy, Sayantan   -   17
Tinetti, Fernando G.   -   49
Tsai, Ming-Shiun   -   31
Tseng, Chia-Wei   -   31
Ul-Haq, Azhar   -   78
Weiss, Jaden D.   -   59
Yang, Yao-Tsung   -   31